i
scare
DAN HICKS # myself

I SCARE MYSELF
DAN HICKS

A Jawbone book
First edition 2017
Published in the UK and the USA by
Jawbone Press
3.1D Union Court
20–22 Union Road
London SW4 6JP
England
www.jawbonepress.com

ISBN 978-1-911036-23-4

EDITOR Kristine McKenna
PROJECT EDITOR Tom Seabrook
JACKET DESIGN Mark Case

Printed in China

1 2 3 4 5 20 19 18 17 16

table of contents

an introduction by elvis costello

The music of Dan Hicks first filtered through to me in England in the early 70s.

I was puzzled and a little unnerved.

Those were earnest times.

Pale young man and woman were hunched over acoustic guitars as if in a confessional. I was a mere apprentice to this trade. Suddenly, here was this MAN; fully-grown, sometimes sporting a moustache which seemed to really belong to him.

Quite aside from his evident abundance of style, he clearly felt the swing and sway of ancient forms, and, rarest of all, he had a sense of humor about it.

It would only become apparent later that there could be such a sting to his wit, his heart and soul sometimes clothed in the disguise of a curious curmudgeon.

It's possible that some people mistook the novel for novelty, but listening just beneath the panache was to be heard a deep cry from within; 'I Scare Myself,' 'It's Not My Time To Go' …

Like I said, unnerving songs from a young man to an even younger man.

What is to be found in these beautiful and fascinating pages is that the license to the carriage which bore Dan Hicks's most soulful, joyful, and painful words did not arrive overnight.

It was not unearned.

He went out looking for clues and cues to the music that he loved. Sought out the mystery and masters at the source, took a couple of stumbles, sipped a couple of concoctions, dreamed an original dream.

It is a consolation to my younger, bedazzled self that Dan Hicks should have written the bones of songs as assured as ''Long Come A Viper' and 'Reelin' Down' during such travels at the age of just twenty-one.

No wonder his later records seemed so impossibly complete.

Yet he went on to hone and whittle that vocabulary until it was like an intercom, breaking through from another room and another time; no fake antique, it all came to vivid life in the moment of performance.

There are lots of people who can point to music on the shelf.

Some like to light candles to it, others seek only to snuff them out.

Dan burned them all brightly, and here is his tale.

ELVIS COSTELLO
VANCOUVER, B.C., CANADA
SEPTEMBER 2016

the california kid

DAN MAKES A LITTLE ROCK GETAWAY,
FOLLOWS HIS MILITARY DAD AROUND
THE STATES, AND FINDS A HOME
IN CALIFORNIA …

I SCARE MYSELF

We won't leave any stone unturned here. We'll get to all the stones, because I'm a giver.

My dad, Ivan Hicks, was born in a small town in Illinois called Gladstone that was right across the Mississippi from Burlington, Iowa—that's where his side of the family was from. My granddad, Jesse—my father's father—was a farmer and was supposedly kind of a mean guy, but I never met him. I did know my grandmother on my dad's side for a long time, though. She lived in Napa and worked as a nurse at a mental institution, and so did her daughter, who was my aunt Cecile.

My dad left the farm in Gladstone when he was eighteen and went off to join the National Guard. After that he was in the army, then in 1947 he joined the air force. He was a military guy, but I never felt like I was raised with any kind of army excessive discipline kind of thing. Maybe it was going on and I didn't know any better, but I wasn't aware of it at the time. Like, the guy Robert Duvall played in *The Great Santini*? There was none of that. My parents were middle-class Midwesterners, though, so there were rules about when I had to be home and so forth, and I had little chores. But I think I had a happy childhood and never thought about being an only child—I never thought I was missing anything, because I didn't know anything else. I don't think I was spoiled like an only child might be, and I was a shy child. I think I'm basically … well … I'd call myself shy all the way up until now.

My dad was in supplies and signal corps, and early on he was a cook. I've wondered whether he dug being in the service, and I think he must've, because after the Korean War ended he was still

7

over there in Okinawa or someplace, so he must've liked not being home—he was away a lot. I really liked it when he came home—that was a great moment.

There's a snapshot I have that he took when he was coming back from Korea or someplace on a big military ship. As it docked in San Francisco he took a picture from way up there on the ship, looking down at the families on the dock waiting to meet their relatives coming in, and you can see me and my grandma and my mom there in the crowd. I remember I used to listen to the radio at ten in the morning, when they'd report which ships were coming in at Fort Mason in San Francisco, and I remember hearing that my dad's ship was coming in one time while my mom was down at the grocery store, and running down there to tell her.

My mother, Evelyn Kehl Hicks, was born in 1910, in Minneapolis, then her family moved to Omaha, which is where she mostly grew up. That's where my parents met. The story is that they were married for about a year before they told anybody, and I guess that was because they couldn't afford to live together—it was the middle of the Depression when they got married. Anyhow, seven years later, I was born in Little Rock, Arkansas. My mom was thirty-one when she gave birth. My earliest memory is of being a little toddler and looking up at my mother and seeing her smile. I also remember being someplace with my parents, and there was a little girl there, and they were saying something like, 'Danny's got a girlfriend.'

Because my father was in the military we moved all the time, and we left Arkansas about a month after I was born. When we were moving around we'd live in these government projects, cheap military housing for government employees. It wasn't that hard on me, all the moving around and changing schools; you know, *here's a new house, this is where we're gonna live, there's a new school a few blocks away.* I have lots of memories of being in new schools, but it never felt strange, and I just flowed with it.

I'm not sure exactly where we went after we left Arkansas, but there are photos of me in Albany, New York. I went to kindergarten in Topeka, Kansas, and when I was five I supposedly sang this song, 'Bell-Bottomed Trousers,' at some kind of school assembly—I was really young when that happened. I went to first grade in Ralston, Nebraska—that was in 1948, the year that Dewey defeated Truman[1]— and at one point we lived in Lomita, in southern California. I remember coming into town and seeing those grasshopper-type oil pumps going up and down.

We moved three times when I was in the sixth grade. In September of 1952 we were living in Vallejo, California, and I got lost in the rain. They had some projects there, and I remember walking by them with a really runny nose. Just before Christmas of that year we moved to Cambria, which is by Hearst Castle and Morro Bay. We were only in Cambria for a few months, but during that time I joined the 4-H Club[2]—my thing was electricity—and I was in a school production of *The Nutcracker Suite.* It was on December 18, 1952, and I was one of the big wooden soldiers.

The fifth and sixth grades were together in one class in Cambria, and this class had a contest where the students wrote a play they would perform for the school. I came up with this play called *Valentine's Day In South America*, and the teacher chose my play. The

9

class was studying Mexico at the time, and these little kids in the play
want to find out what Valentine's Day means. At the end the children
are all at a party, and they sing 'Don't Let The Stars Get In Your Eyes,'
or maybe it was 'Mañana.' Maybe it was both. I might've written a
couple of little poems before that, but this play was an isolated kind
of thing. We also did this thing about the story of Columbus in that
grade that was sort of like a radio play, and I played the part of 'the
innocent bystander'; that phrase always stuck with me.

♠

In the early spring of 1953 we moved to Santa Rosa and finally
stopped moving around all the time. The week before I started at
this new school in Santa Rosa, the kids in the neighborhood told me
that they beat up new kids there, and I remember praying to God the
night before the first day of school that they wouldn't beat me up.
And they didn't beat me up, so I consider that to be the beginning of
my belief in God.

Believing in God has been drummed into me so much in this
twelve-step program that I got that going. In meetings, God is the first
word out of everybody's mouth, and it goes on from there. And that's
something I choose to believe, whether intellectually or emotionally—
it makes just as much sense to believe in God as it does to believe that
we're here on our own. I feel like I'm not alone and something is
kind of watching over me, whether it's my parents who've passed away
or whatever. There have been periods when I didn't pay attention to
any presence that might've been there, but whatever it is, there's a
presence, and I feel like I've been blessed. Somehow I was given the

gift of being able to write and play music, and all the stuff that I have. Clean and sober, you're more accepting of life on life's terms, and you're straight, and you have to deal with stuff.

Anyhow, Santa Rosa. When I was in the sixth grade in Santa Rosa, my class held a talent show, and me and a little girl who lived next door lip-sang to this song called 'Poor Little Josie' that was a two-part thing recorded by Rosemary Clooney and Jimmy Boyd, who was a pretty well-known kid singer at the time. We had a 78 recording of 'Poor Little Josie,' which was about this little bird walking to Missouri because it couldn't afford to fly. We also practiced 'Dennis The Menace.' So, this little next-door neighbor girl and I did 'Poor Little Josie' for the class, and afterwards the teacher said to me, 'I didn't know you had it in ya.' In other words, I was a quiet kid, but I jumped up and did this thing, then I sat back down. I felt comfortable up there doing it.

A lot of movies were shot in Santa Rosa because it had that all-American good look to it. Alfred Hitchcock shot *Shadow Of A Doubt* there in 1943. It was ten years later when we moved there, but some of the stuff you see in that film was still there when we arrived, looking exactly the same. There was a bar in the film called 'Til Two, and I know just where that is. I've been in there. The train station was the same, and there was this great ivy-covered library that was still the same, too.

There's another movie called *Storm Center* that was made in Santa Rosa that stars Bette Davis, who plays a librarian, and they shot it there because of the library. They needed kids to be extras and for some speaking parts, so they contacted the Boys' Club, looking for kids. I was in the Boys' Club, so I went to a meeting about being in the movie, and they told me I had to have a Social Security card, so I got one. I was just gonna be sitting in the library, but when they called our house and needed me immediately I was out, so I missed being in the movie. My mother was in the movie as an extra, though. There's a fire scene at the end where the library's burning down at night, and there's a crowd in front looking up at the flames, *oh, terrible*, and there's my mom looking up at the goddamn fire. She's in there for a couple of seconds. It's cool. She's wearing a little hat, and these 50s glasses, a coat, a typical-looking woman, and there she is.

My mother had little part-time jobs here and there when I was growing up, and she did some volunteer work, but mostly she was at home. I was really close to my mother—I guess she was the parent I identify with the most. She wasn't especially creative, though. I never saw anybody sitting around writing or drawing, and I wasn't a reader as a child, so I don't know how I got involved with writing and music.

My parents had a sense of humor, and they were my first audience, and I'd crack them up at the dinner table. I wasn't the class clown or anything like that, though. As for what played a role in shaping my sense of humor, well, when I was a small child there was an accident and I lost three toes, and the guy who took care of me at the hospital taught me to laugh at life and appreciate what you have. And he took those toes and he put them in a mason jar in some formaldehyde, and there were my little toes floating around in there … and I started writing at that point. Three little toesies in a jar … everything started then. Not really, I'm just kidding here. But as to which funny things I remember from back then? I remember seeing

Spike Jones on television, but he means more to me now than he did then, and I bought *Mad Magazine* when it first came out. It was like a little paperback book then.

The humor thing really began when I started getting up onstage with my guitar by myself. It's a great thing, too, because when you make people laugh, they're probably gonna be on your side. The first thing I say when I start my shows is intended to be funny, and I can gauge what kind of audience it is right away by the response I get. I also try to not repeat myself and to be spontaneous, and for years I never said a line that I'd said before. I didn't care what it was—I'd try to find a different way to say it. I really like it that I can make adults laugh, and I don't take it for granted. But it wasn't something I consciously set out to do like, gee, I think I'll go into comedy.

We lived in a neighborhood of Santa Rosa called Montgomery Village. It was kind of like tract homes, all on one flat level in an area that used to be full of prune trees and different kinds of fruit trees. It was built in the 50s, and all the houses were designed by somebody named Eichmann. It was a new suburban development, so it had baby trees, and there was a central shopping area nearby.

We lived a block from there, and when I was in junior high I met this guy named Kent Benedict who lived near me. He played clarinet in the first band I was in, The Dixieland Dudes, so that's probably how I met him. I can still take Dixieland, too. I like the sound, and all the different guys playing. I've gone to these things they have at hotels on weekends where they have like twenty Dixieland bands performing, and you can walk from room to room, hearing all these different bands. You can get your fill way up to here, though. Dixieland is like bluegrass—you can only take so much—and blues, even, is like that too. You can only take so much. Dixieland is basically jazz, though, and it's got a lot of spontaneity, and I like the songs.

When I was in the junior high band I started listening to Benny Goodman, and Kent and I liked a lot of the same stuff. We were both in the radio guild and we liked the same stuff in that department, too, you know, 'Yes sir, Mr. Benny …' from *The Jack Benny Show* on television. So we teamed up and became Kent & Dan, and we did little parodies on the radio. The radio guild had a radio show for the three years I was in high school; they did shows on the local stations, and I was part of that. We played records and did news announcements, and we did Kent & Dan things like little parodies of TV shows like *You Are There*. I've got a picture of Kent in my bedroom from when we were in high school, and he's got a 78 record in his hand and he looks like a deejay—78s were still around when I was a kid. Kent got out of town right away after high school and he went to Cal at Berkeley. He's a doctor now and lives in Santa Cruz.

I was in a Boys' Club drill team called The Campions that was a precision-marching thing. It was called The Campions because Tom Campion was the founder of the Boys' Club back in the 40s. There was no band, no instruments, and no guns in The Campions, just 'turn left, turn right.' I was in that from junior high all through high school. We did lots of parades and went to South Milwaukee for the national championship competition. First you were in the Boys' Club drill team and you wore blue satin shirts, then you got older and you got into the older-guy outfits, which were striped shirts and conquistador hats. I don't know what it was about it that appealed to me, but I liked it. Maybe I was kind of a natural at it because my dad was in the army—not that he had me marching around. I had to stand at attention in the morning, and we had numbers, and I was number one. No, I'm just kidding.

I was in some sports things, too—mainly baseball—and a little dance band on Saturday mornings. The mentor to that was a guy called Anton Weeks, and he was big time in the 30s, 40s, and 50s. He had a hotel dance band, Dancing With Anton, in San Francisco. I guess you could say I participated in lots of things. I was also in the pep band, and if I look at my yearbook, I see that I was in the Scott Biello Trio, too.

I took typing one year at summer school, but I wound up quitting, and my dad got really mad at me when I told him I quit. He said, 'And I just bought you a new tennis racket!' I said, 'OK, just a minute,' and I went to my bedroom and got the tennis racket and said, 'I don't want this now,' and he knocked me across the room. It was one of the few times he actually hit me. I wasn't ever good at typing.

My parents were country and western fans, so the radio in the house was tuned to that kind of music, and I remember being impressed by some of the novelty country tunes of that period, like 'Life Gets Tee-jus, Don't It?' I liked some of the early 50s pop hits, too, and some of Elvis's tunes when he first started out—'Don't Be Cruel,' for instance. I liked the backup singers, the Jordanaires, although I didn't know I was liking them at the time. They were just part of the sound to me then. I once went by Elvis's place in LA and it was surrounded by die-hard fans, like middle-aged ladies waiting in their cars for a glimpse. That might've been in 1972.

DAN HICKS

I remember seeing The Beatles on *Ed Sullivan*, too. I was caught in the magic of The Beatles. Right then? Everybody wanted to be a Beatle. They were like the goal. Once you saw *Hard Day's Night*, you couldn't not be sucked into it.

When I was ten I got a ukulele, but I didn't play it much, and I wasn't a singer. We went to a Lutheran church and my mom always wanted me to be in the choir, so I did that for a while, but mostly I'd just stand there and mouth the words. Then I started playing the drums when I was in sixth grade down in Cambria. When I was a young drummer, I liked Gene Kruppa, Buddy Rich, Shelly Manne, Dave Brubeck's drummer, Joe Morello, Louie Bellson—I liked a lot of drummers. I remember going to some little benefit for some Dixieland guy who was in the hospital at the Union hall in San Francisco when I was in my early twenties, and upstairs is a band playing, and Shelly Manne was playing the drums, unannounced. There he was, playing. I was thrilled.

Music didn't come easily to me, and I've always worked at stuff. Singing didn't come easy. That chorus-singing thing was when I was pretty young, and when I was in high school I didn't sing at all, even though I was pretty involved in music by then. There was a point with The Charlatans when I was in the band and also doing a little solo work, and I was just able to eke out some kind of living—it probably wasn't until around then that I started considering being a singer. Guitar strumming didn't come easy, and writing didn't come easy, either.

Actually, writing came somewhat easy after I got started, and it was definitely easier than starting out on the guitar. Drums didn't come easy because there was a long time in there that I couldn't read drum music, even though I was in the band. Then when I was around fifteen I must've had an epiphany, because I went to summer music camp at College of the Pacific in Stockton—I think it's called University of the Pacific now—and somehow I got it figured out. There's a lot of working at stuff in this thing—I think an ear can be taught, too. Say you don't have an ear, like I can't carry a tune, I don't even know what I'm listening to—it's just noise with a beat to me, and I don't pay attention to it, and it don't mean nothing to me. To go from that to developing an ear and become a good musician—yeah, that can be done.

I've always had a strong interest in music, but I don't know if I ever decided that I wanted to be a professional musician. It was more a case of, I just sort of kept going. To play the drums or any kind of instrument in places like little restaurants or lodges—which is basically what was going on there at that time—everything was pretty much Union, so when I was seventeen I got my Union card in the Santa Rosa local. It isn't this way now, but back then gigging musicians were all in the Union. I played the drums, and the kind of jobs I played were what we used to call mickey gigs. It was like cornball adult music for dance gigs. Even though I got that Union card, if somebody had asked me, 'What line of work do you think you might go into?' I would've said, 'I don't know.' I don't think I ever thought to myself, *yeah, I wanna be a professional musician …*

♠

DAN HICKS

They filmed some of *American Graffiti* in Santa Rosa, and that's a lot what the place was like. There was all that Friday night going up and down the street in cars, draggin' the main, go a distance, then turn around and drive back.

I got my first car when I was around twenty. It was some kind of Ford that had a green glass top and white leather interior—a really sharp-looking car—but I was not an active guy who dated girls and had a lot of social things going. I was quiet in school, and I was more of an observer of this main drag scene, because me and my friends were band guys, and we just kind of saw all this happening.

I've been to a few of my high-school reunions and nobody acknowledges that I'm a musician at those things. I wasn't a popular kid in school. Now, if I'd been popular … let's just say that if Ted Stayshack had become a movie star? Well, now we got something. But little Danny Hicks? No, I'm still Dan Hicks, senior in band. You don't get the chicks being in the marching band.

Sometime around in there I started going down to the Apex Bookstore, where people sat around strumming guitars and drinking coffee. It was where the 'alternative lifestyle' people went. I was never much of a coffee drinker at that time, but I was there, and there were tables and books, and it was run by an older beatnik guy named Charles Stankey. I was hanging around the Apex in Santa Rosa and I hooked up with two guys, Bob Hoffman and John Brandeberg, and we formed The Redwood Singers. It was two guitars and a banjo, and we were all singing. We didn't get too far, but we had a repertoire.

Around the Apex time there was one particular girl who'd just graduated from catholic high school named Susie Stopple, and we hung out that summer together. She liked Joan Baez and folk music, and we hung out at the Flamingo Hotel pool a lot. How I was making my living during that period, I don't know—maybe I was a part-time busboy? I had to have some kind of gig.

In high school I was not a drinker at all. I was a late bloomer, and that started when I was around twenty and was hanging out at the Apex. I guess that's when I started what people call 'partying.' I was hanging out with the Apex people and drinking a bit, and it was kind of a gradual thing.

I think my first time being drunk was around junior-college age, when I was living with Dick Ziegler up on the Russian River. He was working at a Safeway in Sebastopol, and I was working at Armstrong Park, and we were staying in this kind of tent type cabin. It had a wooden floor and canvas walls and ceiling. I drank some gin, and there was some throwing up involved, and I've never touched gin since. So there was that, and then there was a dance at the Rio Nido.

Say you're going from Santa Rosa up the 101 toward Guerneville, you're gonna start seeing the Russian River on the left, and on the right is what looks like a vacation resort in the Catskills or something, and that's Rio Nido. It's basically a little spot off the side of the road, and there was a nightly dance there, and a lot of kids went there on weekends. They had a little nine-piece band there every night, and it wasn't rock—it was jazzy and nice, and people were still dancing to that kind of stuff then. Kind of a swing thing.

Every Saturday they had two drum sets onstage and there would be a guest drummer and a battle of the drums. One time, one of the drummers didn't show up and they asked if there were any drummers in the house who wanted to play, and my friends talked me into going up there. I wasn't by any means a solo drummer guy—that was not my forte—but I did it anyway. I played a couple of tunes, and I got a free pass for the rest of the summer. This happened on August 5, and every time that date comes around, whoever is near me gets to hear that story.

Anyhow, I was in a car in Rio Nido with a couple of people and I had a can of beer, and a cop came up and we got hauled in. I wasn't drunk but I was underage, and I think they found two draft cards on me. One draft card was the real one, but I also had another one I was working on, and I'd erased some stuff on it. The cop asked me, 'What's this?' and I said, 'This is a draft card that I was gonna change.'

As for the drinking thing … at first you just wanna feel different, and then it gets to a place where you're using it to avoid things in your life. In the AA book, this one guy said, 'Alcohol gave me wings to fly, and then it took away the sky,' and that's a good quote.

From 1959 to 1964, I had one foot in Santa Rosa and one foot in the city, and I went back and forth. I was seventeen when I started at San Francisco State, and during that first year I majored in radio-television-film—what today would be called communications. I lived with this musician guy I knew from high school named Wayne Whitaker who played jazz trombone, and we had a house within walking distance of the campus in the Ingleside area, in a neighborhood called St. Francis Wood. SF State was a bunch of big, industrial-looking buildings, and it didn't have a collegiate look. It looks exactly the same today—just massive, four-story buildings. A little bit of grass and sidewalk, a slope, and down at the bottom of the slope was a men's and a women's dorm that were built while I was there. Not a lot of anything. Just a beige-colored place, and you'd walk from one building to the next and they all looked the same.

Wayne Whitaker was also from Santa Rosa, and we went home on the weekends a lot. In 1960 I moved back in with my parents and went to Santa Rosa Junior College, and got an AA in general education. In 1962 I went back to SF State for a year and lived in the dorm, then I went back to junior college, in Santa Rosa, but I didn't even last a whole semester. I did a lot more hanging out than taking classes, lasting as long as I could living in these Quonset huts they had on campus. Then I went back to SF State and lived somewhere off campus.

I remember dropping out three different times mid-semester. I dropped out a lot and I don't remember the reasons why, but I did have tenacity and I kept going back. My family didn't pressure me about college, and nobody was asking me why when I'd drop out. They figured I was 'college material' and left me on my own. I think my parents knew who I was, and they never tried to dictate what I should do or who I should be. I was more or less independent and supporting myself. It wasn't like I ever quit school permanently—it was always a temporary break. So mostly things were peaceful.

My dad probably would've liked me to go into the military after I graduated from high school, because when I went off to San Francisco State as a freshman he wanted me to enroll in ROTC.[3] It wasn't like that was some kind of thing he thought I'd be pursuing, though, and I think the only reason he wanted me to do that is because there was the draft. It seemed like the army was ahead for everybody, so he said, if you're gonna be in the army, you might as well be an officer.

So I was in ROTC for a semester, and I went along with it, and there was an air-force uniform I had to wear to school every Tuesday, but I didn't like it. I didn't like the regimentation and the 'yes sir, no sir.' They had a flight class, and I liked that, but you also had drill and that uniform. So the second semester I quit, and I think my dad was really mad at me. I never told him how I got out of the draft when that came up, and he never asked, either. I went to college and then joined a rock band, and I never went into the service, and they never said anything like, 'Where's the service?'

My friend Dick Ziegler left Santa Rosa as soon as we graduated high school and went to Cal Poly, in San Luis Obispo. He learned a little bit of folk guitar during his first year there, and when he came back during the summer of 1961 he had a guitar, and I said, 'I wanna learn to play guitar, too.'

During that period my favorites were all the folk people, partly because I could pick their songs up off the records and learn them. I think of folk music as urban people trying to get real, and one of the great things about it is that you can play it yourself. That's one thing. It also makes it possible for you to do something you'd never done before, which is sing—you can find out how you are as a singer. And I liked hearing it. That's the main reason I got attracted to it. I liked the sound.

In those days, the big thrill was to go to open-mic hootenannies and get up there and play, and hang out in the dressing room with all these other people who liked the music you liked. I have a newspaper clipping about my first solo performance in San Francisco, which was in 1963. I was so nervous that my fingerpicks fell off of my fingers, because I was sweating so much. It was a hoot night at a small club with ceilings so low that you had to bend down to get in, and I remember Dino Valenti was there in this little dressing room they had. He was a very unique singer-guitar-entertainer guy, and was a real local star on the North Beach scene. He was kind of the Tony Bennett of folk, now that I think about the sound of his voice. I didn't know him that well but I liked him, and I remember saying hello to him with my fingerpicks falling off.

I went to a few Monterey Folk Festivals, and I remember being there in 1963. I definitely saw some people there. I saw Jerry Garcia playing banjo, and a solo guy named Michael Cooney—he was good, but I don't think anything ever came of him. Doc Watson and The New Lost City Ramblers were there, and Peter, Paul & Mary. I didn't like the schmaltzy songs, but I liked some of their stuff. Mance Lipscomb was good, too. He was one of those guys who got discovered after living in obscurity for many years, one of those blues-singer guys. You have to be black to make that sound—a white guy can't make that sound—although Mose Allison can sound like a black guy. When I first heard Bob Dylan it was in Monterey in 1963, and he automatically became my favorite folk singer. He was a solo act that was good. He jumped around a lot and was kind of funny, and everybody liked him for sure.

Folk music was big for me then but I still listened to jazz, too. There was a place in San Francisco in the late 50s where people like Dave Brubeck would play called the Black Hawk, and my friends and

DAN HICKS

I used to go to the city and listen through the door, because we were too young to get in. Then there was Bop City, at Post and Buchanan, which opened at two in the morning and went until six. When I was in college there were a few times when me and a friend or two would stay up until two and go down there. It was all black guys, hard bop guys, and people would wait their turn to sit in on these big jam sessions with lots of guys playing tenor saxophone. I took my sticks one time and I had more moxie than chops. I was kind of a dumb, skinny white kid, around nineteen years old, and I go in there with my sticks and I wait all night to get my turn. So I finally got my turn, and they laid these songs on me—like really hard stuff, fast 3/4 time, you know, *keep up with this.* They were messing with me.

♠

I wrote my first song the same year that I started playing guitar, which was 1961. I was just learning to strum 'Michael Row The Boat Ashore' and a few other songs like 'Irene Goodnight,' 'Red River Valley,' and 'Alberta Let Your Hair Hang Low.' On Labor Day weekend I rode up to Lake Tahoe with two of my friends from Santa Rosa who were both twenty-one. I was still underage, though. I was in Harrah's at the nickel machines, and a cop—or a house dick, to use the parlance of the time—came over and asked me how old I was. So they took me into an office, then they took me in the sheriff's car to the local jail, which was a few miles down the road in Zephyr Cove. They told me, 'You're underage and you're in a gambling hall and that's not good. The fine is $25, so pay it and you can go.' I didn't have $25, and I don't think my friends did, either, but they raised the money somehow, and I was bailed out. On the way back to Santa Rosa I was in the back seat of the car with my guitar, and I started strumming something about Zephyr Cove jail. That was my first song, and that's how it came about. I never performed it because it wasn't that good.

Officially, my first song is 'How Can I Miss You When You Won't Go Away?,' and I was in junior college when I wrote it. There was this guy sitting by the cafeteria whose name I can't remember, and he said, 'Why don't you write a song called "How Can I Miss You When You Won't Go Away?"' So I tried to do it, and I got my first song. I dug it, and I kind of had a person in mind when I wrote it. I don't know if I'm ready to reveal her name in this particular chapter. Well, OK—her name was Alma Freeman, and some people knew this, and they said, 'Hey, is that song about Alma?' There was this girl named Alma who was hanging out, and I guess she was kind of an acquaintance of mine, but not a girlfriend, and I guess she liked me, but it was one of those situations where the feelings weren't totally mutual, and I wrote that song about the situation.

There's was a guy around then named Joe Nixon, who was a deejay at the one country station in Santa Rosa, and he was a cool kind of overweight jolly guy, and he was older and was a professional country guy, and we all liked him. I played him the song, and he said, 'That's good, keep writing.' That was encouraging.

america
the
beautiful

A VW BUS, FOLKNIKS, AND A
MORMON DRIVER …

Dick Ziegler lived just a few blocks away from me in Montgomery Village, and he was my best friend. I met him in junior high because he was a trombone player in the school band I was drumming in, and we had lots of common music interests. He was in my class at Montgomery High School, and his dad would drive up in his truck when school got out and drive us home.

Dick was a little shorter than me and was a handsome guy who wore glasses. He was naturally tan and had a good build—there was surfing down there in San Luis Obispo, and he looked athletic. The whole folk thing was just beginning to boom with The Kingston Trio and Joan Baez, but it hadn't hit national television yet. Dick was singing a few folk songs but he wasn't a singer, and I hadn't really started singing yet, either.

I spent the summer of 1962 in Guerneville, working as a maintenance guy at the Armstrong Redwood State Park on the Russian River. Dick was there too for part of the summer, and he and I lived in a little bungalow. We liked The Kingston Trio and we learned a bunch of their tunes, so we started strumming together, and that's when we started getting the Dick & Dan thing going. I was learning everybody else's songs, and it was a real labor of love, and it was just the greatest.

So we got some striped shirts and entered a couple of talent shows in Rio Nido. I have a list of the songs Dick and I used to sing; we did some Kingston Trio songs and some other more esoteric stuff, and as time went by my awareness of other types of music broadened. Folk music is very earnest, and the sardonic stuff didn't start coming in until I started writing songs.

DAN HICKS

Members of the bohemian crowd at the Apex were always saying, 'I'm going to New York, gotta go to New York!' That was the refrain for the hip people, because you were gonna change your life, you were gonna go to fuckin' New York. It was almost like a threat, like, *you better not be here next week, because if you're going to New York then go!* Maybe one sixteenth of the people who said they were going actually went.

In the summer of 1963, three of the guys who hung around the Apex, Tom Candrion, Gary Maulm, and Tom Whitaker, actually went, and when they came back they'd grown their hair long and had done a pretty hip trip. We dug that they were able to do it, so the following summer Dick & Dan said to themselves, 'Let's us go this summer.' I personally didn't have any big fantasy about New York—it was just a place to me—but I liked the idea of the trip. So, after my classes at San Francisco State ended in May, I went down to San Luis Obispo and stayed with Dick for about a month in a trailer park where he was living, then we took off around June 20 and got back maybe ten weeks later. The trip we did was even cooler, because we played music while we traveled.

♠

Dick cashed in the sports car he'd been driving and got this Volkswagen van, kind of a grayish, tan car—used, of course. We had like a mattress bunk thing, this two-level setup, and we slept in the car just about every night, one guy in the bunk and the other guy on the floor. We had Dick's upright bass and our two guitars, and Dick had some money. I had very little, and he was occasionally able to loan me money, which was a good thing. After we got home I paid him back.

Dick had a rule that there couldn't be any weed in the van. He was a Mormon, and he wasn't a zealot or anything, but he had that upbringing, and his brother was going into missionary work. So, between me and Dick, I guess I was the wild one. There was one point where Dick and I had some weed in the Volkswagen van, but it wasn't there for long, and we were hardly drinking—we didn't indulge in much of anything, because we were just digging being out there in new places, playing music.

Dick did most of the driving. The only time I drove, the car broke down—the car broke down thanks to me. We took the southern route east and the northern route on the way back west. We went through Arizona, New Mexico, Texas, New Orleans, Mississippi, and Memphis, and then headed north. Our idea was, we were gonna make our way across the country by playing music and getting paid for it. We left from San Luis, and that first night we got to some little town and went into this bar, and we told the guy we'd play some music for a small amount of money—and we did it! We got $5 apiece and thought, *this is a piece of cake!* Well, we didn't do it again for quite a while.

We got to Texas and went to this coffeehouse in Houston that was co-owned by some guy from Santa Rosa. We auditioned, and he said, 'OK, you can play tomorrow night—you're hired,' and we were there for a few days. They liked us because I did a little fingerpicking, and we weren't run of the mill—we had cool songs and were a little bit ahead of the curve.

DAN HICKS

Guy Clark was one of the local musicians there, and I met him at this place called the Coffeehouse. He had a tune I liked called 'I Got Mine,' and when I told him I liked it he wrote down the words for me. He was just a local person then—his name didn't surface until a few years later—and he was a friendly guy. Everybody supported each other in the folk thing, and we all learned things from each other. We were all digging the fact that we liked this kind of music and we had the same heroes.

I wrote a few songs while we were on that trip but we didn't really do my songs. We were trying to sound like folk singers rather than, *here I am, I'm a songwriter*. I guess you could say that was the incubation period for my songwriting. ''Long Come A Viper' came during that period, and I wrote 'Reelin' Down' while we were in Houston—I wrote it on July 2, which was Dick's birthday. I guess you could say that's autobiographical, because the first line is, 'Didn't get to ramblin' 'til I was twenty-one,' and I was twenty-one at the time, and I was out there with Dick, going from town to town.

Even though my family had lived all over the country, that was the first time I'd left California as a grown-up person. So, yeah, I'm reelin' down. That was the third or fourth song I wrote. I hardly ever wrote a song in one sitting. It's never like I can say, OK, between two and four I'm going to write. No. Usually I would write a little bit of something, then lose interest in it, and come back to it later. Or I get tired of it and feel like my brain is racked, I can't do this anymore. But I'll come back to it.

After Texas, we headed for New Orleans, but nothing happened there—we didn't play there. Then we went from New Orleans up to

Mississippi. We were driving through there right after those three SNCC volunteers were killed, and we later found out that they were driving Volkswagen buses.[4] We were in a Volkswagen bus and had long hair, and we knew what was going on there. I was a college kid, so I knew why those students were all there.

When we got to Memphis we found a guitar store, and that led us to the scene. We made all our connections by gravitating to where the folk people were, and somehow we always found them. It wasn't jazzers or rock'n'roll people hanging out in clubs drinking and dancing—it was a whole other kind of people, and they were totally focused on the folk stuff. You didn't hear much about politics in these places; it was about music.

There was this house in Memphis, a big place with lots of rooms, that was full of these folk types, and somehow we made our way to that house and parked our van outside and slept there. At that point people were making pilgrimages to the South to find old blues guys—this happened with Mississippi John Hurt, for instance—and bringing them back into the world, and these southern blues guys became folk idols. John Fahey and two friends of his named Bill Barth and Henry Vestine were going down south doing that kind of thing, and they found Skip James. So those guys were with Skip James at this house, and they were on their way from wherever it was they found him to the Newport Folk Festival, which was where we were headed, too.

Skip James was a slight old guy, he was probably around fifty, but he seemed old to us. And he was Skip James. He did a lot of picking around the kitchen table there, and he was really good on the guitar and the piano, and he had a cool, high voice. He wrote some song that Cream did later—like 'Feel So Bad' or something—and he became pretty famous because Eric Clapton did his song.[5]

One day I walked by his room, the door's open, and he's trying to get his T-shirt on and he was having trouble. I went in and pulled down his shirt for him, and he said thank you, and I continued on my way. I saw him play in a little place during the time I was in Memphis. It was like, OK, Skip's gonna be down at the Sunny Rainbow tonight and we're all going down, and then not long after that we saw him at the Newport Folk Festival.

While we were in Memphis we went swimming at a public pool one afternoon, and the person who admitted us to the pool asked us if we were 'nigger-lovers.' Not only could black people not go swimming there, people who *liked* black people couldn't go swimming there. And we looked different. We wouldn't stand out now, looking the way we did, but at that time and at that location we did stand out.

Memphis was still in 1949, even though it was 1964. One of the girls at the pool asked me if I was Troy Donahue. I'd always been into black music because I always loved jazz, and I loved some blues, too. Not a lot of R&B for me yet, at that point, but I liked Josh White and Big Bill Broonzy and Lightnin' Hopkins—so yeah, I love black people. When I was seventeen or eighteen I went with Wayne Whitaker to the Longshoremen's Auditorium to see The Count Basie Band, and I think we were the only white people in the place. It was good, too.

♠

I SCARE MYSELF

We were passing through New Rochelle, on our way to New York, and the car breaks down. The repair was gonna take a couple of days, so we decided to take the subway into the city. We came out of the subway station and there we were on the streets of New York—the busy streets, the vastness of it all, it was cool. We gravitated toward the Village, and in those days they had what they called basket houses; anybody could come in and get onstage and sing, and at the end of their three- or four-song set, they would pass a basket among the people sitting there—who were probably people like you who didn't have much money anyway.

Café Wha?, café this and café that, Gerde's Folk City—there were a lot of places with music—and the Kettle of Fish was a little restaurant where people gathered. So we played there and passed the basket—you'd walk around yourself with the basket. Whether or not you got any money had to do with how good the last song in your set was. Actually, not only was it dependent on how good your last song was—it came down to how good your last note was. If you had a big finish, then there was clapping. We did a tune called 'Grizzly Bear' that was one of our big numbers.

While we were in the city I think we slept in an abandoned car. We found some cars parked and we got in one of them and slept with our guitars. Dick didn't have his upright bass with him—I don't know where it was. One day we were on the street and somebody came up and told us we could get a free spaghetti dinner and a place to stay if we joined this picket line of people who were picketing so people who worked at all these coffeehouses could get minimum wage or something. So we picketed, and then it was time for our free

33

meal, and we went up to this apartment on Bleecker Street where there was a bunch of people sitting around.

We have our free meal then suddenly somebody says, 'The cops are coming!' I don't know why the cops would be interested in coming there, but back in those days the cops were always coming. Then somebody says, 'If anybody's got a record or any warrants out on them, they should leave,' and everybody starts talking, like, 'I'm wanted over in Brooklyn, I'm wanted for being in a gambling house in Tahoe, in Jersey there's a pick-pocketing charge against me, so yeah, I'll leave.' Dick and I went out the back door and ended up sleeping on some floor.

So, yeah, I had some adventures. I was standing outside a coffeehouse and Dick was off somewhere else, and this girl came up to me and said, 'Hi, Ricky,' and I said hi. So she thinks I'm Ricky, and I start playing along—she was kind of hot, and I'm not telling her I'm not Ricky. So we walk over to Washington Square Park, and she says, 'Gee, your voice sounds different,' and I said, 'Well, I have a cold.' Then we sit down on a bench and start kissing, and it was kind if unbelievable. Then we went our separate ways! I never told her I wasn't Ricky.

We went to the World's Fair, and because Dick was a Mormon we went to the Mormon pavilion and saw a movie about what it's like to go to heaven. All the Mormons are up in heaven, and you go up there and get back with your family. There's your uncle Jim—he's over there in a white robe, and you can walk over to him and say hi. Dick's brother did the whole missionary thing and went to the Belgian Congo, and he's still a big guy in the Mormon church.

34

I SCARE MYSELF

We were in the city just a few days, and then we headed for the Newport Folk Festival. We saw quite a few people at the Newport Folk Festival, and we were very glad to be there. We were big fans of The Kweskin Jug Band, Buffy Sainte-Marie, Odetta, The Country Gentlemen, Big Bill Broonzy—they had these afternoon workshops where we saw a lot of amazing people. It was kind of like idol worship. There's Geoff Muldaur—wow! 'Coney Island Washboard Baby'—all those first songs the Kwewkin Band did. I think Maria Muldaur was in the band then.

There was housing for the artists nearby, and somehow we got wind of something happening at this house where all the blues guys were staying. Lightnin' Hopkins, Jesse Fuller, and everybody—they all stayed in one place. I was a big Jesse Fuller fan. He did this sort of fingerpicking I liked, and his songs were right up my alley. He didn't do 'I Got Mine,' but his songs were kind of like that, almost like songs from a minstrel show. 'San Francisco Bay Blues,' of course, and 'The Monkey Said To The Baboon,' and a bunch of other tunes I like. His voice was great, and the fact that he was this one-man band who could make the whole sound himself was a big feature. The lone cat.

Anyhow, we're over at this blues house one afternoon, and for some reason there was nobody there. We were wandering around, thinking maybe we shouldn't be here, and we went up one floor and there on the landing was Jesse Fuller's whole setup. He had the little high hat, and what he called the *fortella*, which was kind of like the thing the organ player uses to play bass notes with his foot. Jesse Fuller had a similar kind of thing for his bass sound. He had an amplified acoustic twelve-string, and of course he had a kazoo

35

and the rack with the harmonica—which I think is probably where people like Bob Dylan got that idea. All us folkies had a harmonica rack at some point and I had one, too.

So we're there on the landing, and I sat down at Jesse Fuller's set, which was one of the highlights of the trip. And then we left.

We went from Newport to Cambridge, which was another place the folkies gravitated to, and you'd often find groups of them living in a house together. Somehow, again, we found one of those kinds of houses in Cambridge. Jim Kweskin and some Kweskin Jug Band types were living there, and Harvard Square was within walking distance from the house. On the lawn there during the daytime was more picking and jamming, and I saw Taj Mahal sitting out on the green, playing with a group of people who'd gathered around. He wasn't any kind of name yet—he was just doing it, and he was worth listening to. He was kind of a standout guy because he could play and sing so cool.

We went to some snooty-wooty place in the Hamptons and tried to play in the town square and were told we had to leave. They weren't allowing this kind of activity in this particular neighborhood. Then we got to Martha's Vineyard and visited Lowell Levinger. He was a guy from Santa Rosa, a little younger than us, who was kind of precocious—I say that because he was very good at playing instruments, but he was younger than us, so that makes him precocious. His nickname was Banana, and he wound up being in The Youngbloods, which was one of those groups that had one good song and 720 shitty ones.

Anyhow, we knew Banana was there, and he had a little guitar shop in Martha's Vineyard with his pot-smoking, fingerpicking buddies, and they were all there, too. So that was a little scene on Martha's Vineyard, and they knew everybody in Cambridge, and they knew the Jim Kweskin people, and there was kind of a jug-bandy thing going on. I played washboard with them at one gig. Banana had some weed, so there was a little bit of pot smoking there.

There was one point when Dick and I were on our way back west and we were in Kansas. It was seven o'clock on a Sunday night in some little town, and we decided to stop and go window-shopping. There was nobody around, and we're walking along, looking in shop windows, and this sheriff comes along. We're lookin' like hippies. We were growing our hair and were kind of rag-tag, wearing sandals with no socks—to him we were definitely looking like hippies. He asked us what we were doing, and then he said, 'I'm gonna walk you guys back to your van and check it out.' I said, yeah, you know, we may be thieves, or maybe even killers! The guy did not laugh. I said, 'Don't you have a sense of humor?' And he said, 'Not with some people.'

We took the northern route home and stopped off in Omaha because my mother was from there, and her brother lived there with his wife, Frieda. Uncle Phil. We spent the night at their place and got snapshots of Uncle Phil and Aunt Frieda with two longhairs. We tried a little playing on the street there, and stood in front of the van with a sign that said 'California or Bust.' I can't remember how that worked out.

And then we got home. We experienced things we'd never experienced before, and I think I got closer to what my lifestyle was gonna be on that trip. Dick was confronted by Cal Poly when he went back to school. He was studying to be a teacher, and there must've been some incident where he had some weed. I don't know how they knew about it, but the powers that be at Cal Poly told him not to smoke any more weed if he wanted to be a teacher, and I guess he obeyed, because he was a grade-school teacher all his life. I went back to San Francisco State and singing down in North Beach, and things happened fast.

In 1965, in a period of one week, I graduated from college and took the draft test. I did everything I could do to not be in the service. I told them I was gay, I wet the bed, I took dope, and I scored as low as I could on the intelligence test. They gave me a deferment—1Y, they called it. Then, that same week, I went away with The Charlatans and everything kept going from there. I had to go back and take another draft test the following year, though. I took a bus over there, and I may have eaten a bunch of weed. I was late, and everybody was in the little classroom taking the test, and I was standing there. Some guy came down the hallway and I heard him say, 'Where's that dud?'

in
head
first

TRIBAL STOMPIN' WITH THE
CHARLATANS, THE RED DOG, THE
HAIGHT-A, AND THE SCENE …

DAN HICKS

George Hunter grew up in LA, but I don't know anything about his LA life, because it never came up. Supposedly he was studying architecture or something, and he was definitely an artist kind of guy who could draw and all that stuff. So, Hunter comes to San Francisco and meets Richard Olsen, who was in a class with George's girlfriend, Lucy Lewis, at San Francisco State. She was involved in dance, and I think Richard was, too. Richard could sing and read music and was really a musician. He was actually a clarinet and sax player, and he was good on those things, but I think he learned the bass because the band needed a bass player, and he wanted to be in the band. And he could look the part, too.

George did the hiring based on how you looked, and he wanted Richard in the band. I don't know if Richard was too happy, though. Yeah, he could've been a little uncomfortable about his self-image, and I can say that because I was suffering with that same insecurity at that time. I brought in this song, 'Moody Richard,' and he got pissed off because he thought it was about him. Anyhow, Olsen's on bass, and he and George got together and formed what they called a conceptual rock group, whatever that is.

Mike Wilhelm was a friend of George's from LA who played a lot of harmonica, and when Mike lit upon San Francisco he joined the band, and then Mike Ferguson joined next. Ferguson was argumentative and one of those complainer types—you know, 'Do we have to move the piano now?' He was kind of a dark character who always marched to his own drummer, and he was a somewhat limited musician who did kind of a Chuck Berry piano style. Then Sam Linde was hired, then fired, as drummer.

40

Wilhelm was with a girl who was living in San Francisco but sometimes went to Santa Rosa on weekends, like me. For some reason I knew her, and early in 1965 she was giving me a ride to Santa Rosa and she mentioned that her boyfriend was in a band that was looking for a drummer. Rock had never really been my thing, but let's say you're playing a hotel or a party or something, you might be playing a little country here, and there would be a little rock in the mix, too. Early on, before The Charlatans, I played a lot of gigs like that, so I felt OK in the rock world, because as a drummer it's one of the kinds of music you play.

I was in my last semester at San Francisco State at that point, and I had a job at a clipping service for television and radio. I worked in an office from six at night until midnight, five nights a week, and my job was to monitor newscasts and talk shows, looking for possible mentions of the clients who hired this service. Like, if there was a sit-down strike at the Bank of America mentioned on the radio, you made a note of that for Bank of America. You taped everything, and I had all these tape recorders going all the time.

It was during that period that I started going over to George Hunter's place on Downey Street and rehearsing with The Charlatans on a regular basis. At the early rehearsals I was mostly just trying to come up with drum parts that would work with the songs we were doing.

During this whole period of my last year of college and being with The Charlatans and having that job I was dabbling in smoking weed. And it so happened that at this job I had I was by myself in a big office building that was all closed down, except for me. I didn't always smoke weed at work, but one night I guess I smoked a little bit because I was in a mellow state, and I got all the radios tuned to the jazz stations and went to the bathroom.

I'd already given notice that I was leaving this job to the lady who hired me, because I knew I was going up to Virginia City with The Charlatans. She never shows up at night, this boss lady, but suddenly there she is. She looks at me and says, 'Is this what you do?!' I had another week on the job, and she said, 'You don't have to wait to go—you can turn in your key now!' So yeah, that was the getting-fired thing. I walked out of there and took the bus home.

♠

One problem with the band was that George wasn't a real musician—he was more like the manager and image-maker. He tried the guitar and Autoharp a little bit, but he mostly played tambourine, and I think it upset him that he couldn't play. He wasn't a singer, either, but he was important, and we put up with him because it was his idea and his thing and he was a strong, colorful guy. He was connected to all kinds of people in the arts and poets like Michael McClure. The rest of us didn't know any of those people, but he and Lucy knew all of them.

The image thing was important to George, maybe because he couldn't play anything, and I kind of dug that we had an image. Before we'd even played any gigs, Richard, Wilhelm, and George already had the image thing going—George was into those stiff, old-timey collars that you had to hook on, the long, Dutch boy hair, black jeans, Beatle boots, black vests. Those guys dressed like that even when they were just hanging out, so they were noticeable. They looked like English rockers of the period, and we had a distinctive look when we got onstage. George ran the band, and he could be a little dictatorial about the look, but he let me slide on the stiff collar thing. He didn't make me do anything, but he'd make a comment if I came up with something that seemed wrong to him.

One of the partners in the Red Dog Saloon in Virginia City, Nevada, was a guy named Chan Laughlin who lived up around there. I think Chan managed a coffeehouse in Berkeley that was way pre–Red Dog. Anyhow, he came down to San Francisco looking for people he could hire for this bar he was opening—he needed bartenders and carpenters and cooks and all that. He went to Seattle looking for people to hire for this thing—for whatever reason there were people from Seattle who were part of the Red Dog scene, too. The story goes that he saw some of the guys in The Charlatans on the street in North Beach and he asked them if they were The Byrds—there weren't a whole lot of people who had this look yet, so I can see why he thought that. They said, 'No, we're somebody else.' Chan told them about this thing in Virginia City, and because he liked the way they looked, we were hired, sound unheard, and were told when we needed to be there.

We'd never played anywhere before we went to the Red Dog, but Mike Ferguson and George had the logo and the artwork and the poster finished way before the gig happened. George is a graphic artist, and Mike was an artist who did a lot of drawing, and he drew this poster announcing that The Charlatans were gonna be at the Red Dog. It's around ten by fourteen inches, what you'd call a broadside, and it's an old-timey thing with drawings of each one of us in little frames. This poster is known as 'The Seed,' and they're worth a lot now.

The poster said that we'd be opening at the Red Dog on June 1, but we didn't make that date, so George took the original and added more things and changed the date. It was Ferguson who drew this thing, though. Ferguson painted the sign that hung outside the Red Dog, too. It's a big, circular white thing with a Red Dog in the middle of it—not a whole dog, just the face and front shoulders of a gnarly looking dog.

So we went up there. The place was owned by Mark Unobsky, this guitar picker, kind of a blues acoustic guy with a rich father. Somehow Mark ended up in Nevada, and he'd been around that area for quite a while. Mark and his friends decided they needed more room to goof off in, so they found a place and named it probably after that place in Alaska called the Red Dog. Before we got there they knocked some walls out to make it bigger—I played there a few years ago and it's smaller now—and they were still working on the place when we got there. There were plenty of these carpenter-guy construction cronies of Mark Unobsky's around, and they were hippies.

I had a room upstairs—you just kind of grabbed something, and my room had a big water heater in it. It was funky but I didn't care. We all lived upstairs, and the place was staffed with hippie types—not scroungy good-for-nothings, just people with long hair and a certain style. They were hippies in philosophy and attitude, not 'can you spare a dime?' A bunch of pretty cool people—and I still think that. It's just a thing you have with all those people. Those were the formative years, you know? It was a really neat place to be at that age, and that summer.

We played six nights a week and had good meals every night, multiple courses, and we'd sit at a big long table. We had access to the kitchen, and we could go in during the daytime and get a sandwich or something. We got a hundred dollars each, which was pretty good. Yeah, it was pretty goddamn good. I liked being the drummer of The Charlatans and dug being part of the scene.

Every now and then The Charlatans would have a manager, and at that point we had this guy named Phil Hammond. He got to go to the Red Dog, too, and he got paid every week and got food and lodgings—he was like part of the band, and he supposedly wrote press copy, but it seemed like he didn't do anything while we were there. I don't know what he did, but he wasn't playing every night like we were. The band was always really George's thing, and eventually Phil started having conflict with him. George probably started not liking him, and then swayed Richie and Wilhelm against him. I saw that happen; George would start making fun of someone and soon they'd be on their way out. Rock'n'roll isn't always nice.

We hung out there for a few days before the place opened, and one night not long after we got there they opened up the place for the employees and we played our audition. We all had rooms above the saloon, and during the afternoon, before the audition, a guy came along and said, 'Do you want your acid now or after dinner?' Everybody in the band, and all the Red Dog employees, took acid the night we auditioned. We played a little bit for a while, then we started trading instruments, and things got real disorganized and crazy—we were just up there, loaded and playing. We got the job.

The Red Dog was a scene and nobody was in a hurry. Initially, everybody in that scene was a middle-class white kid; there were later developments that changed that, but at the beginning it was middle-class, white, fringe people. Chan could've been behind the bar—he was definitely one of the main characters and a host kind of guy, and what exactly he did I don't know, but he was always talking. Hard drugs weren't really part of that scene; during the period I was in The Charlatans, I don't remember anything like coke being around. There was weed and a little acid, a benny here and there, but nobody was snorting copious amounts of speed and staying up for days. People didn't drink a lot on that scene, but booze was there, of course, and that's when I really started drinking.

My friends then were the guys in the band, and I had a few friends from San Francisco State. I've kind of always been a loner and kind of a solitary, not naturally gregarious guy—I guess you could say I was Moody Richard—but I socialized pretty good in the rock band milieu. But I was mostly trying to figure out what I was gonna be when I grew up, and I wasn't really involved in the politics of being a hippie. There were little fringe benefits that came with being part of the hippie scene, maybe on the sex or dope front, but I was mostly focusing on the music and trying to make a living.

A few weeks after I got to the Red Dog, this girl named Candi Storniola showed up, and she became my girlfriend. She was around eighteen—pretty young—and was one of those people who came down from Seattle with some friends, you know, *let's go for a ride*, and

46

she ended up staying. So we hooked up and she started staying in my room, and we ended up going back to the city together.

The Red Dog was dark on Monday nights, and a lot of people would take LSD on their day off. I didn't know who Owsley Stanley was until I got back to the city at the end of that summer, and I don't know if he supplied the acid at the Red Dog—acid can come from different places.[6]

Once, really early in the morning—like 8am, which was early to us—everybody in the band, and some of the people who worked at the Red Dog, took acid and went to Pyramid Lake, which is near a sacred Indian burial site, and we stayed there all night. I wouldn't recommend acid to anybody, but that was a pretty good experience. By the time we got there, the acid was going strong, and at one point I got off by myself and this image of Gabby Hayes came to me—I don't know why he came to me. I guess I've always liked all that cowboy western stuff. I remember talking to a friend that day and telling him that I didn't want to be the drummer in a rock band, and that what I wanted to do is sing and play guitar. That might've been some kind of turning point there.

There was a contingency of the local townsfolk who didn't like the hippies being there, and at some point a tombstone appeared on the stage that had the word 'Charlatans' etched into it. This could've been the Clampers. There's some fraternal, a-hole lodge type thing called E Clampus Vitus, and they all wore red shirts. There was a big deck on the second floor of the Red Dog that looked down over the street, and we'd sit up there and watch when there was a parade in town. Apparently, the people there had lots of reasons to celebrate because there were lots of parades, and they'd have camel races and shit. There was this one parade with all these Clampers carrying rifles loaded with blanks, and when they saw us sitting up there on the Red Dog deck they went ape-shit and starting firing on us. One time a Clamper came into the Red Dog with bug spray and started spraying us. That was a transitional period, and those were the days when there was a lot of hostility toward hippies and longhairs. So, yeah, there was a small opposing faction, but most of it was friendly. Carson City, the capitol of Nevada, wasn't that far, and the governor came and danced at the Red Dog.

The Charlatans had no singer, really. There wasn't a good front voice, so we took turns getting out in front, and even George had his turn at the vocals. I wasn't that good a singer then, and I wasn't a front man yet, either. When I moved up to the guitar and did some singing in The Charlatans, I didn't step up and do Chuck Berry tunes—I did old-timey songs like 'Somebody Stole My Gal' and folky stuff like 'On The Road Again.'

♠

The P.H. Factor Jug Band was kind of a cool, established band from Oregon, and they'd come down on Saturday afternoons, and I would sit in with them. And there was a girl named Lynne Hughs, who was from Portland or Seattle; she was a folk-blues type singer who was pretty good, and she started sitting in with The Charlatans. I don't know how she got to the Red Dog, but she became Chan's girlfriend, and she was the bookkeeper and was a waitress, also. When we got back to the city after the Red Dog summer, she

TOP LEFT 'Senior Character Day—won last prize!'—D.H. **LEFT** Dan with a fellow member of the Santa Rosa High School Band, c. 1959. **BELOW LEFT** 'Formal Dance Date—first car—very cool Ford.'—D.H. **ABOVE** Dan with his parents, Ivan Hicks and Evelyn Kehl Hicks. (*Note: captions marked 'D.H.' were written by Dan*.)

AUG · 64 · ©

SEP · 64 · C

SEP · 64 · C

SEP • 64 • C

OPPOSITE Dan with Dick Ziegler in Omaha, Nebraska, and the pair with Dan's aunt Frieda during their cross-country trip, September 1964. **ABOVE** Dick and Dan on the road. **RIGHT** Dan and Dick performing in a Santa Rosa hootenanny.

OPPOSITE The Charlatans in Haight-Ashbury, 1967. *Left to right*: George Hunter, Dan Hicks, Richard Olsen, Mike Ferguson, Mike Wilhelm. **LEFT** Posters for a Charlatans gig at the Avalon Ballroom in 1967, and an early Dan Hicks & The Hot Licks show at the Fillmore Auditorium. **ABOVE** An early promotional shot of The Charlatans, taken in Golden Gate Park, San Francisco.

53

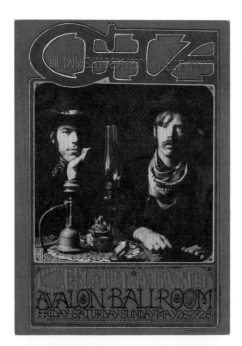

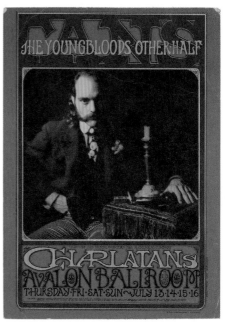

ABOVE AND LEFT A set of promotional postcards advertising The Charlatans' gigs at the Avalon Ballroom in July 1967, featuring band-members Mike Wilhelm and Dan (*top left*), George Hunter and Richard Olsen (*left*), and Mike Ferguson (*above*). OPPOSITE Mike and Dan.

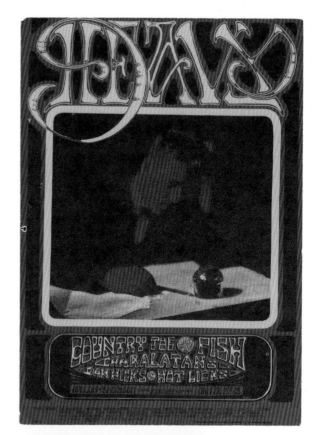

RIGHT A poster for a 1968 Avalon Ballroom show featuring both The Charlatans and Dan Hicks & The Hot Licks. BELOW The Charlatans at the Red Dog, Nevada, 1965. OPPOSITE The original lyrics to Dan's ''Long Come A Viper,' which he wrote in the mid 60s.

(Long Comme Viper)

I. D I was standing on the corner with my feet in my shoes
       Twistin' my brain how da pay my dues
   My ~~bucket~~ was empty & o' my ~~war~~ number 1 booze
   A long come a viper and I blew my ~~blues~~ blues

X G It got so I was feelin' no pain
       Just a groovin' behind that Mary Jane, yeah

D   " " "
       with all my might now, really up tight now
A⁷ ~~this is the day~~
       ~~a letter is to plates to make sure fly~~
       Just a blowin' that stuff away out night

II. A long come my chick, come my little dolly
    She was out a walkin' her big fat collie
    Golly, Miss Polly says your lookin' mighty jay jolly
    There aint none left I really mighty solly

G   " " "
D   the way I'm talkin', it may be a sin ___ I thinks
A⁷ ~~But do the~~ it If it's cool enough I'll do it again
    I really hate to hang you in dissipation
    But blowin' this stuff is my full time occupation
D   If you don't get the point, I'm doin' up a joint
    ~~If~~ it don't click now, I'm doin up a stick now.

IV Beddle am bam, puttin' on a scam
    ~~the~~ a Re Bop a Sat lemme hear that scat

    If

RIGHT Dan and Candi Storniola at a Grateful Dead jam and pool party. ('Nice Hair' — D.H.) BELOW The Charlatans poster known as 'The Seed.' BELOW RIGHT The Charlatans onstage in Golden Gate Park during the Summer of Love. OPPOSITE The Charlatans, 1965.

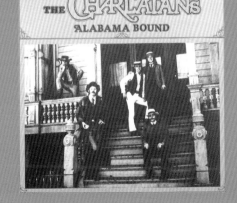

OPPOSITE The Charlatans in Golden Gate Park with a group of unidentified girls in 1965. ABOVE An outtake from the photo session for the group's first single, 'Alabama Bound.' RIGHT Artwork for the single.

I SCARE MYSELF

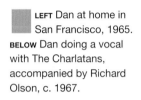 **LEFT** Dan at home in San Francisco, 1965.
BELOW Dan doing a vocal with The Charlatans, accompanied by Richard Olson, c. 1967.

RIGHT A flyer for The Charlatans' gig in the Crystal Ballroom on board the H.M.S. Portland, March 1967. **BELOW** The band on deck.

was a guest singer at some Charlatans concerts, and she was later in a band called Stone Ground. She was still up there with Chan in Silver City when she died a few years back.

Also on the Red Dog scene was Marlon Melvin, a cool cat, tall, thin, good-lookin' biker guy who came through and later became a deejay at KSAN in Reno. He was one of these guys who'd traded with the Indians and had belts with old turquoise and buffalo nickels. Some of the guys on that scene had been to places like Taos—places I didn't know anything about. And there was this short, blond character named Zela Mortimer, who always had a little gun in her garter. Why did she have a gun in her garter? Because that's what you did. She got a little black kitten, and I said, 'Why don't you call him Shadow?'

Tom Donahue was a deejay in San Francisco, and he had a label called Autumn Records with a partner named Bob Mitchell. Donahue had a few things going and had some pop band, maybe The Beau Brummels, so he was having some success with these local long-haired bands. He wanted to see if we were gonna be one of them, so during that Red Dog summer we took the train down from Reno and he took us into Coast Recorders to record a demo of a few songs.

Those were the first recordings for The Charlatans, and Donahue was using Sly Stone as producer. All I can remember about Sly was him running around from one instrument to the next, showing us how versatile he was and that he could play all these instruments. I got the impression he was trying to impress us, like, *dig me*. It was kind of rinky-dink. Sly was also a deejay then, and he had a pretty cool radio show. He was kind of sexy and he'd get girls on the phone, and he was good with the writing thing.

65

DAN HICKS

Anyhow, Tom had picked out some songs he wanted us to record—I think 'Leavin' On A Jet Plane' was one of them—and he thought maybe they could be hits. We may have tried them, but either we couldn't do them or we wouldn't do them—whatever the problem was, I've never heard any recordings that were produced that day. I don't think any of The Charlatans thought we had one particular song that should be a hit, or could be a hit, unless it was 'Alabama Bound.' I think Mike Wilhelm brought that song to the band, and it got on some *Rolling Stone* list of the greatest rock'n'roll tunes of all time. I don't know how great it was, but it definitely belongs on that list.

♠

When that summer ended, a lot of people from the Red Dog moved back to communal places on Pine Street. I never lived on Pine Street, but there were two addresses on Pine Street that were the popular addresses of the people involved, and one of them was where George and Lucy lived. Some other people lived there, too—maybe Bill Ham, the light-show guy—and it was one of those big old houses.

There was another place about a block and a half down the street where Ellen Harman lived, and she was one of the Family Dog people—maybe some other Family Dog people lived there, too. Ellen had a mixed Australian Shepherd dog, and at one point her dog had a litter of puppies. Ellen came to me and handed me this white and tan Australian Shepherd puppy, and it was definitely a royal dog, being an offspring of the Family Dog. I called him Fetch, and I had Fetch until I moved to Mill Valley. He was with me there for quite a while.

The Family Dog was started by four people—Jack Tollen, Luria Castell, Ellen Harman, and Alton Kelly—and they put on the first few dances. Then they decided they didn't want to be concert producers, and the name lay dormant for a while. Then various people took up the name to do events—possibly Rock Scully, who was more or less the manager of the Grateful Dead with Danny Rifkin, and maybe even George Hunter—so those guys may have been the Family Dog for a while.

Somewhere along the way, Chet Helms got the name going, got a logo, and started putting on dances at the Avalon for real. Chet was a neat guy. I think he'd been a student at San Francisco State, because I used to see him going there on the trolley. He was easygoing, and he was also one of the first longhairs. I always liked him.

A lot of stuff happened in a really short period of time. There were so many people panhandling on Haight Street that I made a little button that said, 'Can you spare any gall?' 'Cause I thought it took a lot of gall to be constantly hitting people up for money. Most of the people they were out there asking didn't have any money, either.

I do remember doing angel dust at one point during that period, and I had some experiences later on with that drug that weren't too good—it's just too strong, that stuff. I was in my early thirties when I did that.

Early in 1966, I went to the Trips Festival at the Longshoremen's Auditorium, and the Trips Festival was trippy, man. I saw Neal Cassady there, mumbling. He was a very frenetic guy standing there, and his hands are moving and his body's moving, and then he said something on the mic, and I thought, *they're gonna let this guy up onstage?* I don't think I was on LSD, but I remember Ken Kesey getting up on the stage. I liked his book, *One Flew Over The Cuckoo's Nest*, and I liked the fact that he was a well-known guy who was successful in his field and decided to become an outrageous character. That appealed to me.

At the end of the summer of 1966, Tom Donahue got tickets for everybody in The Charlatans to see The Beatles at Candlestick Park, which was the last show of that tour—and of their entire career, as it turned out. They came on in an armored truck that drove them out to second base where there was a stage, and they all piled out. You could hear them, too. We'd been told that their playing was always drowned out by girls screaming, but we could hear them.

How were they? The Beatles were fine.

So yeah, a lot happened.

♠

All the bands on that scene felt a kinship with each other. We played gigs together, lived in the same neighborhood, we knew each other from scenes before then—coffeehouses, and San Francisco State, and different places. I definitely felt that. I don't know what all those people thought of The Charlatans, because we had a mixed reputation. We weren't that commercial, and the other bands were kind of getting more success, shall we say. We may've been as ambitious as bands like the Jefferson Airplane, but we weren't as well directed, and I think the musicianship was probably better in some of the other bands. The Charlatans had a lot of worked out stuff, but we were sort of a jam band.

I knew Janis Joplin before she was in Big Brother, and I always liked her. She was kind of a rough, tough beatnik, but she was nice, and I thought she was a good singer. I met her in the Folkie Coffee Gallery in North Beach. I sang some song there, and after the show she asked me to give it to her, which I did. I don't know who wrote it, but it's one of those old folk Dixieland things called 'Wild Women Don't Worry,' and it's a good song. She lived in the Haight when the fame started happening, and I remember going into a store on Haight Street and she was sitting on the floor looking through all the magazines she was in. She was cool. Janis partied, but she was never too lucky in love, and men treated her not so good. There's some story about her having played someplace where she was paid forty grand, then she walked home alone. Stuff like that. Her end was an OD, and that's always a risk when you're taking heroin, because you don't really know what you're taking, or how strong it is.

I saw the Dead a lot. I can't really dive in and say, 'Wow, that's great,' about any of the stuff by the Dead, but they had a certain sound and a certain function. You take those big halls and you get a band going, and there's some energy there—yeah, they could do that. And big personalities, too. Jerry Garcia was like an icon, and he kind of deserved to be—I thought he was a good guy. As for what the regular, Joe Schmo Dead fan on the street thought of him, I think it was kind of a hero-worship thing. I can listen to some of their stuff on the radio now if I accidentally tune in to it.

I remember Marty Balin being in a folk group called The Town

DAN HICKS

Criers before the Jefferson Airplane got together, so I knew he was good. They had a good sound, that kind of soaring thing, and always did a good show. I remember seeing them at the Matrix, which they partially owned, in the Union District. I wasn't quite in love with Grace Slick's voice. I thought she had a voice, but she didn't do the right thing with it. She had a strident voice, and I would've liked to hear her sing some other kinds of songs, but I liked the Airplane.

I liked Quicksilver Messenger Service, too. Those long jams on 'Mona' or 'Who Do You Love'—those things kept going forever, and they never bored me. Maybe I was on the dance floor while they played—that was part of it. I'd go to the Avalon when I wasn't playing, and I liked to dance. I liked John Cipollina, and I knew Dino Valenti—I don't think he knew me—from folk joints.

Moby Grape was somebody's idea of a commercial band, and they were pretty good performers. They did this thing where all of them—maybe four guys in a row with guitars—would all come up to the mic at the same time, then they'd back off. It looked good, and they were the flavor of the week for a while, so there might've been some unspoken envy going on. Here's this band getting all this action—they released like five singles at the same time, which was pretty unusual. They had this guy in the band who was kind of nutty, Skip Spence, and he was the first drummer in the Airplane, then he turned into some kind of guitar player. Moby Grape did a reunion gig a few years ago at Golden Gate Field, and they were awful. Awful! When they reform these bands, there's maybe three of the original guys, then they bring some other people in, and it's usually awful.

70

The musicians on that scene were generally good, but only to a point. Most of the bands had maybe one or two people who were good, and the rest of the people were being carried. LA probably had better musicians, because it was slicker and more commercial down there—that's kind of what we thought of them. We're funky and raw and real, and they're commercial and phony.

Some people have said that The Charlatans paved the way for country-rock, but all that country-rock stuff came out of LA, and I don't think the musicians there had even heard of The Charlatans.

Most of the people in those San Francisco bands came to rock out of folk music. When I got in The Charlatans I didn't lose interest in folk music—I haven't lost interest in it to this day—and I continued doing solo folk gigs around San Francisco. I did get a little more interested in rock'n'roll when I was in The Charlatans, and I started listening more to Top 40 because we wanted to be successful, and we felt like we were in the running and were a band who could have a hit. There were a few Top 40 things that caught my ear, like 'Laugh Laugh' by The Beau Brummels. I liked that. Still, rock'n'roll was never really my thing.

♠

Candi and I came back to the city together from the Red Dog, but then we broke up, and there was a period there when I was wishing I could get back together with her. The first place I remember living after the Red Dog was in a room on Haight Street, off of Divisadero Street. I was living there when The Charlatans played the Matrix and the Longshoremen's Hall, and the next place

DAN HICKS

I lived could've been on Ashbury, right off of Haight. I lived upstairs in a flat, and there were maybe three or four people I knew from San Francisco State living in the building, too. I took to living with a bunch of people OK—it was part of what you did then, because you needed cheap rent. By the time I got back from the Red Dog, my parents knew I was some kind of hippie, but they didn't wanna ask. I don't remember getting any hassle. I probably should've been in the army then, according to them, but they knew I wasn't in the army.

So, Candi showed up at the place on Ashbury, and we both stayed at that address for maybe a year. Then we moved out to a place on Noriega Street in the Sunset District, and that wasn't real good. I was living on Noriega when the Human Be-In took place, and I only lived a few blocks away. I could've walked over, but I was working on some songs, and I guess that event wasn't a priority for me.

I lived in an apartment that was underneath a house, like in the basement, and that was kind of weird. I wasn't a real happy camper then. It was when I was living on Noriega that I struggled for the first time with the feeling that something serious is going on here, I'm isolated and I'm on my own, and no one else is experiencing this thing I'm experiencing, and I don't know what to do about it except try to keep living with it. That was the first time I got that down. I was at a low period in my mental makeup, and I was having kind of loss-of-self feelings. I was experiencing that stuff, for sure.

Then we lived in a place on 12th Avenue for a brief period, and it was pretty straight out there. Candi started painting all the walls these really dark colors, and the people who owned the place got pissed and we were asked to leave. Then we moved to a house on Delmar, which was the last place I lived in the city before moving to Marin. I don't know why I moved so much. It wasn't some kind of nomad thing—it was probably because I was with Candi, so I couldn't just live in a room somewhere. We needed a kitchen and all that.

After the Red Dog summer, the other Charlatans found places and stayed put, partly because they'd do all this decorating and put a lot of work into how their places looked. They'd collect all these things, and put up velvet drapes and Maxfield Parrish pictures—yeah, that vintage thing was how we lived. Your old lady would spend time getting all that together, but the guys dug it, too. I kind of developed a sense of style and an appreciation for old-timey stuff and art nouveau from those people. I don't know if I would've been hip to that stuff if it weren't for those guys.

The Charlatans mostly played the Bay Area, and we didn't tour much at all. We wanted to tour more—we were a rock'n'roll band—but it just wasn't happening. It always went pretty well when we got out there, though. Funky, long hair, electric instruments and a backbeat—it was enough. We played Portland and Seattle and Vancouver, and Denver was as far east as we got. There was a place in Denver called the Family Dog that was kind of a satellite of the San Francisco thing. I think Chet was doing the Family Dog by then.

We went down to LA to play the Cheetah in Santa Monica, and I remember this chick I ended up with on that trip. I remember her name, but I can't tell you that—I guess you could say I left a trail of bodies behind me. Anyhow, she was definitely hot. She told me that she was once at a party and Rock Hudson fell back off his chair trying to get a look at her. It didn't matter that he was gay—she was a good-looking woman. Yeah, the Cheetah. That was pretty much the Cheetah experience for me.

During that period, Luria Castell went down to LA and was in some LA club like the Trip, and she saw Erik Jacobsen. She knew who he was, and that he'd been producing hits for The Lovin' Spoonful, and she told him, 'You gotta check this band called The Charlatans.' So he checked us out and signed us to his management company, Faithful Virtue, then got us signed to a label called Kama Sutra that was co-founded by this guy named Artie Ripp.

We recorded three songs for Kama Sutra, again at Coast Studios, and Erik produced those recordings. He'd be telling us whether we had a good take or not, and we all went along with what he said because we thought he was a big shot. We recorded a Buffy Sainte-Marie song called 'Codeine,' and we wanted to release it as a single, but they thought it was too wild or something. Instead, they released our cover of The Coasters' song 'The Shadow Knows,' which none of us wanted. It flopped, and Kama Sutra sold us to Kapp.

George and Richard and Wilhelm were a particular type of person, and me and Ferguson were a different type of person. George and Wilhelm and Richard sat around the kitchen table, smoking jays, and they came up with all kinds of ideas, including just how popular this band was. Those guys did have a bit of a 'we're hot shit' thing going, and I was more or less an observer of this. So, Artie Ripp was interested in the band, and these guys from New York came out to meet with us at George's and talk about stuff. George and Richard thought, *we're gonna fix these guys, we're gonna outsmart them, because we're a lot hipper,* but it didn't happen that way. Those cats just held their own, and they weren't overwhelmed by The Charlatans.

So, there's Broadway and Columbus in North Beach, and that's where most of the topless places were in San Francisco then. Down the block, off the main drag, was Varni's Roaring Twenties, and The Charlatans were the house band there for six months. It wasn't like all these hippie bands got jobs at topless places—that wasn't the case, and it was unusual for a band like us to be playing there. It was a classy place, old-fashioned-looking, with gilded stuff and stained-glass windows—you know, fancy-schmancy. There were always two topless girls dancing on the bar, and in another section there was another girl dancing on a table, and there was another topless dancer on a platform right next to the drummer, which was me. So there was always some girl right next to me dancing topless. Every half hour or so, a topless girl would swing through the place on a swing suspended from the ceiling, and that's kind of where I started my MC work. I'd jump up from the drums and introduce the girl on the swing.

I didn't date any of the girls at the club because I was with Candi then. I tried to not be faithful a couple of times, but I was unsuccessful. You know, hormones—remember them? One night Candi was at the club, and to my surprise she got up there and danced topless for a while. It was weird. I didn't get upset, but I wouldn't say I was proud of her. She wasn't drunk, either. She's a very outspoken person, this Candi person, and I think she did it just for a laugh. She was a pretty good looker, so she had a lot of self-confidence. We just played our regular repertoire at the Roaring Twenties, and the band was probably at its best during that period because we were playing so much.

DAN HICKS

During the summer of 1967, when we were playing at Varni's, we went into Golden State Recorders in San Francisco and recorded some songs, and they came out pretty good. I know we did 'Alabama Bound' and 'Sweet Sue,' and a song George and Richie wrote called 'I Always Wanted A Girl Like You,' and my songs 'My Old Timey Baby' and 'We're Not On The Same Trip' and 'How Can I Miss You When You Won't Go Away?' They're on a British Charlatans compilation that was released in 1996.

Not long before I quit The Charlatans to do The Hot Licks, Ferguson was asked to leave because he kept not showing up and was a kind of difficult guy. His attitude got too lax, so we got another guy from LA to play piano. Like I said, from time to time there was an acting manager for The Charlatans—it was never really anybody but George, but occasionally somebody stepped in. So one of these manager guys and I went down to LA, and it may've been on Hollywood Boulevard, I don't remember for sure, but we saw this guy playing ragtime piano in a pizza joint. For some reason we knew to go see this guy, and we did. He was real good—he played like Scott Joplin and was into the old-timey music, and he probably had the right vest—so we asked this guy, his name was Pat Gogerty, if he wanted to join the band, and he said yes.

Pat came up to San Francisco and joined the band, and he was living in George's front room, and nobody had any inkling that the guy was gay. But George found some kind of homosexual tape, something real private with Patrick talking about his homosexual experiences—and George wigs when he sees this. So he tells the rest of the Charlatans, and we were all shocked. I didn't have that much experience myself personally with gay people, and it was as if he'd told me the guy was spying for Russia or something. That attitude was an innate part of the consciousness of that period.

So now every-fucking-body in the band knows this guy is gay, but he doesn't know we know. It wasn't like he was trying to hide it—it just never came up—but it got to where he would leave the room and there would be a joke about him. Not good, not good. We didn't fire him, but he left the band because he wanted to move back to LA or something, but you can hear him on a couple of the Charlatans tunes. He was a good guy, and the band was kind of unkind to him, but it wasn't a good time to be gay. If you're gonna be gay, now's the time to do it. Don't wait, though. It could get ugly again.

At the beginning of 1968 we did some more recording in Sausalito, in some funky place at one of the Gates—Gate 5, maybe—and Gogerty played on those songs. A fiddle player named Hank Bradley, from The Cleanliness & Godliness Skiffle Band, was brought in, and we did some pretty good songs. I did an old vaudeville tune called 'I Got Mine,' and we did 'East Virginia' and 'Steppin' In Society.' And that was the last time I was in the studio with The Charlatans.

♠

You can put up with more when you're in your early twenties, as we all were, but eventually the scene with The Charlatans got pretty uncomfortable. I remember taking a break to go to the men's room during some show we were doing, and I could hear the band playing in this big hall, and I thought, *what am I doing with these people?* The music must've sounded shitty, and now and then it would get to me. Even now, when we try to do a reunion, it's not so good.

I guess you might say this whole unhappy atmosphere descended on The Charlatans, so I got out of there and started playing with more reasonable people who were more interested in the music, and kind of leading my own thing. What's the phrase, cooler heads will prevail? They weren't upset when I left because I was doing pretty darn good with this acoustic band that I had. Then Wilhelm and Olsen pulled this ruse and said, 'Hey, we're quitting and this band isn't happening anymore.' George said, 'OK, I'll turn in my black vest,' and then a week later Wilhelm and Olsen reformed the band. They were just trying to get rid of George, and were really in there rehearsing with some new guys, but the new lineup never really did much. And I was out of there by then.

sizzlin'
licks

DAN HICKS

I was a jazz aficionado from the get-go, and I liked the jazz feel. That's my taste; it's what I identify with, and what speaks to me. I didn't really seek out rock'n'roll as music I wanted to listen to, because I think rock'n'roll is inherently kind of jerky-sounding. It wasn't like I expected The Charlatans to have a smooth, cool sound—they were pretty much what I'd expect a band like that to sound like. I knew what the thing was, so it wasn't a surprise that everything I brought into The Charlatans ended up as a rock song, and lost my linear, kind of floating feeling. I wanted to be a lead singer and try writing more songs, though, so at the same time that I was in The Charlatans I was also doing a little bit of solo performing, singing with the guitar.

Around then I started thinking about getting people who could back me up, and making the thing as jazzy as possible. There was a little country stuff in there that couldn't be avoided because of the way I play guitar and the nature of my voice, so some country swing was part of it, too, but I wanted it to be mostly about jazz. I didn't approach this thing thinking, *this is the sound I want.* It was more like taking the ingredients I liked, putting them together, and seeing what came out. It was my particular kind of guitar strumming, my style of song, my way of singing, and a couple of girls singing with me. A lot of musicians have used that male/female vocal thing—Tex Beneke, Ray Charles, lots of people—and I liked the vocal sound of Brazil '66, so I was thinking along those lines.

In the fall of 1967, I got a gig at the Avalon, and the first thing I tried as far as working with girl singers was with my girlfriend, Candi, and her two cronies, Paulette and Bryce, none of whom were singers. They were more interested in what they were going to wear, and were

80

into the glory of the thing—you know, 'We're cool chicks and we're goin' up on the stage,' because they were all good-lookers. One was half black, one was half Asian—they just looked great. I worked on an easy call-and-response thing with them, but they were never really gonna do it, and they chickened out on the day of the gig.

I wanted to add a bass and a lead instrument to this thing, so I started working with a bass player named Jaime Leopold, and David LaFlamme, who played violin, and that was really the official beginning of The Hot Licks. When I first started thinking about having a band, I made a list of names that might work—the Ragamuffins, different names—and The Hot Licks was on that list. 'Hot licks' is an old jazz phrase I first heard in a Glenn Miller tune from the 40s called 'Juke Box Saturday Night.' So, Jaime, David, and I played that Avalon gig as a trio, and that was the first time I used The Hot Licks—I started using that name before I had any girl singers.

David LaFlamme was more or less the first member of the band. He could play a kind of swing violin, and there were very few guys around who could do that at that point. There are quite a few people playing jazz violin now, especially with the Django revival, but back then there were hardly any of them, especially on the local level where I was. I don't know how I got the idea that my stuff would sound good with violin, because I didn't really know Django and Stéphane Grappelli's music at that point, and nobody had a violin back then except for country and bluegrass bands, and Jim Kweskin, who had Richard Green during the later days of the Jug Band.

David was a nice guy—pretty good-looking, too—and he'd worked in restaurants walking around playing the violin. A strolling violinist. A lot of guys like David had a classical background, so he had that going on, too, and he was pretty talented.

David had been in a band called The Electric Orkustra with Jaime Leopold, and Jaime was a smart, funny guy. He was the person in the group that I was closest to. He was always very supportive, and a good friend.

A guy named Bobby Beausoleil, who was known as Bummer Bob, was also in The Electric Orkustra, and he joined the Manson Family not long after that. I remember him being around—he always wore a top hat—and we were all surprised when he wound up where he wound up.

I learned a couple of years ago that a guy who is a contemporary of mine today had been in the Manson Family, and had also been convicted of murder. He was a friend until I found out about all this. It was too creepy, knowing this stuff about him. He spent fifteen years in prison. He happened to be a musician, and Charlie Manson liked that about him.

During that time, toward the end of 1967, David, Jaime, and I made a set of demos, more or less through some people with The Kingston Trio, and a lot of that stuff wound up on *Early Muses*. The F.W. Kuh Memorial Auditorium was a place in North Beach, at Green and Union Street, next to the Spaghetti Factory, that was run by Joan Reynolds, who was married to Nick Reynolds, who was in The Kingston Trio. Joan and Nick took an interest in me, and under their auspices I made a twelve-song demo at Trident Studios, which was on the bottom floor of the Columbus Towers. Joan and Nick made little two-song discs and wrote a letter of introduction, and they sent them around to various record companies. Joan took the liberty of writing different bios for the three of us—'His parents were missionaries in deepest Africa during World War II, and he learned to play thumb piano'—she just kind of made stuff up.

I didn't get to know David very well, and it was kind of a brief encounter—he was in the band maybe six months. He was on quite a few gigs, though, and he played a gig at the New Committee Theater, in April of 1968, that Ralph Gleason wrote a really positive review of in the *Chronicle*. That was important for the band. Not long after that, David left to form his own group, It's A Beautiful Day, and they did an album for Columbia with a bunch of songs David wrote with his rock'n'roll piano-playing wife.

George Hunter was also a graphic designer, and after The Charlatans broke up he formed a thing called Globe Propaganda with another guy, and they did the cover for the first It's A Beautiful Day record. George was a big Maxfield Parrish fan, and he would plagiarize a little bit—he'd find an obscure old artwork, then have some guy on his team repaint the image. He did the cover for the first Hot Licks record, *Original Recordings*, and the cover for the Quicksilver Messenger Service album *Happy Trails*.

♠

In 1967 my parents got divorced after thirty-three years of marriage. It was kind of weird to be happening to people their age—my dad was sixty-two and my mom was fifty-eight—but I kind of took it in stride. It wasn't like I was totally self-absorbed, but for whatever reason, I wasn't affected real deeply. Maybe I expected all this to happen. I don't know. They had a difficult marriage, and going back to when I was eleven years old, I can remember my dad telling me that there might be a change, and that he was gonna leave. I remember them fighting with each other a lot—when they fought, I was just glad they weren't yelling at me. Anyhow, my dad got very dissatisfied with my mom and finally initiated the divorce, which is something he'd wanted to do for quite a while.

When they broke up, my dad got a place in Santa Rosa, then not long after that he started traveling. He was just out there driving around, and in 1968 he went back to Illinois. It was there, when he was visiting everybody, that he died. He had a little bit of a heart history, and he died of a heart attack. My aunt Cecile called me when I was still living with Candi on Del Mar, and she said it like this: 'I have to tell you that your father, Ivan Hicks, passed away.' Like I wouldn't remember that his name was Ivan Hicks.

So I cut my hair and went back to the funeral, and met a lot of people I didn't know who were my relatives. The local Veterans of Foreign Wars did a twenty-one-gun salute at his funeral—seven guys fired three shots each—and they folded up a flag and gave it to my grandma. My mother was always kind of bent out of shape that she didn't get the flag. She made a real big deal out of that—yeah, she could go on and on about it.

After the funeral, I drove my dad's car back to San Francisco. A lot was going on then. The Democratic Convention was happening in Chicago, and I remember thinking I could go to the convention if I wanted to, but I didn't go.

After my dad left my mom she was kind of down, and I felt

sorry that she was having a hard time. She was living in this trailer in Santa Rosa, and she died there in 1974. I was living in Mill Valley then, and her neighbor called and told me my mom had died—I think this neighbor actually discovered the body. The story is that she had a flammable nightgown on, and it caught fire from a gas stove. I didn't press for details, but she could've died right there on the kitchen floor.

I had to take care of the funeral arrangements and all that, because I was the only person around to do it. I had to get rid of all her stuff and close down the place where she lived. I gave a bunch of stuff to the Goodwill, and I gave her hi-fi set to the woman next door who found her. I kept a few pieces of her furniture, and had some rings that belonged to her, but I gave them to a girlfriend I hooked up with later named China White, and she hocked them for dope. There was a funeral in Santa Rosa, and I got this guy I knew from the Campions Drill Team named Richard Hernandez to blow a little trumpet. I got him to blow taps for us.

After the funeral service there was a burial an hour later, but I was late for that because I stopped off at the bar on the way there. I was late to my mother's burial because I was getting an extra drink down at the bar. I stayed pretty loaded through this whole thing.

I think I'd experience her death a lot differently now than I did at the time when it happened. The night before the funeral, I was in a hotel room, scanning the TV, and I hit on some local news saying, '… and The Hot Licks. Mrs. Hicks was known to dabble in the occult.' I have no idea what that meant. The only thing I can think of is that she liked to go to different churches. My mother must've been an interesting woman—I guess I should've paid more attention. I saw her the weekend before she died, and we'd had a good time together. Sometimes we didn't get along and she'd get mad at me about stuff and our meeting wouldn't go well. I was glad I'd seen her and we'd gotten along.

♠

I was with Candi for three years, but the last year of being together we weren't real together—people would stay out all night, and the other person wouldn't ask any questions. This kind of shit. It was getting bad.

During that last year before we split up, while I was still in The Charlatans and just getting The Hot Licks going, she started flirting with Boz Scaggs, and I suspected she was being unfaithful. At one point, her mom got sick and Candi wanted to go see her in Seattle, so she bought a plane ticket and said, 'I'm going to the airport.' When I told her I'd give her a ride, she said, 'No, I've got a ride.'

I watched her walk down to the end of the block and saw her get into this car—I think it was a Mustang—and it was fuckin' Boz. I got in my car and followed them to the airport, and when he was walking her toward the gate I show up. I'm yelling that I was going back to the house and break everything—there were a few neat things in the house, too. Boz didn't do a thing, because he figured this scene was her baby. I respected Boz as a musician, and still do, by the way. Candi was Irish-Italian, and she liked to raise her voice so there was a lot of yelling, and that was pretty much when we broke up.

Then another thing happened with that. There was one point after I'd moved out when I needed a suitcase that was in the house where I'd lived with her on Delmar Place, so I went over there one afternoon. I knocked on the door—KNOCK-KNOCK-KNOCK-KNOCK!—but there was no answer, so I went around to the back door, and KNOCK-KNOCK!

From the back porch of that house you could look down on the back porch of the Grateful Dead's house—an interesting extra fact. Anyhow, the back door was open, and I went into the bedroom where the suitcase was, and they were both in there in bed. I said, 'Don't mind me,' and got the suitcase out of the closet and left. I was over her by then, and as far as I was concerned, Boz could have her.

By the end of 1967, the Haight had turned into a tourist thing, and there were lots of people and panhandlers on the street. It turned into an ugly scene, and there was bad stuff going on with the police with tear gas, and lots of bikers, and places being boarded up. Then the Methedrine element came in, which made it rougher, and it got sort of unbearable.

There's a film called *Revolution* that's basically footage of the Haight, and I'm in that. I was sitting on a park bench with my guitar, which is something I never did, and a film crew came up to me and said they were filming the flower children and asked if they could film me. I told them I didn't know if I was what they were looking for but that I had a song, so they went and got their cameras and filmed me doing this song 'He Don't Care,' which they used in the movie. The lyric is, 'He don't care 'cause he's stoned,' so they cut to some guy stumbling around, then they cut back to me.

DAN HICKS

The scene in the Haight that had been there at the beginning no longer existed. The changes were happening at the same time as my breakup with Candi and getting the new band going, so I moved on. I was glad to get out of the Haight, out of San Francisco altogether, and that's how I got started in Marin. I was looking for a place to live, and there was a houseboat in Sausalito called the Blue Goose for rent on Gate 5 that was owned by a guy named Mike Considine. Many of the houseboats along the dock at Gate 5 were flat-roofed, which made for a good place to sit and catch the sun. Sometimes the girls went topless, but it was kind of a private scene, tucked away.

Right around the corner was a cool folkie place called the Lion's Share that was also owned by Mike Considine—people like Jack Elliott played there, and it was mostly an acoustic place. I don't know if it was open all night or what, but around three in the morning they'd have breakfast, and I remember the smell of bacon and eggs in that place. It was a little joint with a tiny back room and a tiny kitchen, and it was across the street from a movie theater that's still there.

I thought, *oh, man, I'm moving to Sausalito and I'm gonna have a place to play right here, and it's gonna be great,* but the night before I moved in, the place burned down. They moved the Lion's Share out to another location in Marin County, out by San Anselmo, and it continued there for a long time. I remember being there for some benefit, and backstage they had nitrous oxide tanks that got you stoned for a few seconds. Everybody was backstage wanting this stuff, practically pushing people aside so they could be next. It's a gross life. I just threw that dope story in to make it colorful here.

88

I didn't know much about the scene at Gate 5 until I moved there, but it was really cool—it was like the last frontier. Gate 5 was definitely a good period for me, especially when I was forming The Hot Licks and living the bachelor life. This was a pretty vast area. I don't know how many houseboats there were, but there were a hundred people, more or less, who were part of this scene. There were these guys at Gate 5 called the Red Legs, and at one point the county was trying to close down Gate 5 because of the sewer or health problems or something, so the Red Legs got this armada of boats together and pushed the cops away.

All the houseboats had names. Mine was the Blue Goose, and right next to me was Fortune Cookie. The metal base of the Blue Goose was an old LDSC, which were the army landing craft they used in World War II. Those things that rolled onto the beach on D-Day—those were LDSCs. The rent was fifteen dollars a month, and it wasn't big—it was small, real small. You had to go down a little ramp to get on it, and there was a little boat right next to it.

After maybe a year, Mike Considine sold this boat to Erik Jacobsen, so I moved to another boat called the Bret Hart. There was a big sign on it that said, 'The Bret Hart Sanitarium. San Joaquin Valley County.' China White was staying on a nearby houseboat, and I met her when she was sunbathing on the dock. She started living with me on the Bret Hart and joined me on a steady basis.

China was smart, but she didn't go to school. She was an only child. Her dad left at an early age, and her mother always thought the dad would come back. There were years of this for her mom. We spent most of our time hanging out—we'd just hang out and groove—and

DAN HICKS

she worked as a waitress down at the Trident Restaurant. The Trident was downtown on the water in an old boating club, and it became a hoity-toity hippie scene. I spent a lot of time there.

♠

At the end of 1967, Jaime got arrested for pot and had to go serve six months in jail. He was in jail from January until June of 1968, and he was in jail when I moved to Marin. So I got another bass player named Bill Douglass who had a wife named Mitzi who sang. Mitzi and Bill Douglass were very serious people, and I think they're still that way. I saw Bill playing with Mose Allison a couple of years ago. Bill's a short guy who likes to sit down, so he had two cones where his feet would go, and he faced straight ahead to the audience with one leg on each side of the bass, and his feet on these cones. And he's got a crew cut. Who has a fuckin' crew cut? And he fuckin' never smiled. It was the weirdest look, I swear to God. I didn't speak to him that night, although I would've if he'd been right next to me, but I didn't seek him out. I was thinking about going backstage and saying hello to Mose, but I'm glad I didn't, because I heard he was in a bad mood that night.

I'm not real big on visiting dressing rooms. I went to see Kurt Elling not long ago, and after the show the guy who ran the jazz festival said, 'Hey, come on, want to go backstage?' I said, 'He doesn't know me,' and I didn't go. I'd prepared a couple of nice things to say in case I wound up face to face with him, though, and I did like the show that night. I'd had reservations about Kurt Elling because he's kind of pedantic about his whole jazz thing—he's an educator—but I

90

was glad to see that he'd cut his ponytail off. He had the Count Basie Band behind him, and he held his own and did good.

Barbara Cook is a Broadway singer who does my arrangement of 'Don't Want Love,' and I once went to see her at a club. After the show I was on my way out, thinking, *oh, man*, making a clean getaway, and this person comes up to me and says, 'Barbara would like to see you backstage in the dressing room.' I said, 'I pass.' I can't take the pressure. I'm too shy and I don't know what to say.

Anyhow, I see Bill Douglass's name now and then.

Mitzi Douglass had a friend named Patti Urban, so they became the singers, and they were pretty good. Patti was like a jazz singer who'd hung out in the Fillmore and done jazz gigs, and her voice had a good feel. Mitzi had a nice high voice, and she was tall and skinny. Patti was normal height and weight, so they had sort of a Mutt and Jeff look. Patti left after just a few months and changed her name to Padma, so I guess she'd joined some kind of group. Padma later married a black guy who was a high-school educator kind of guy, and they moved to the heart of the white supremacist thing in Idaho.

Mitzi and Bill were into Gurdjieff and were in a group led by a guy named Alex Horn, who was a kind of guru guy. On weekends they'd go up to someplace in Sonoma County as part of whatever it was they were doing. At some point they were told to sever all past relationships, so they quit the band—they actually left a little note on my door: 'We'll be moving on.' That's how they did it.

So I called this Alex Horn guy and asked him, 'Why are these people in my band cutting off their relationships?' He said, 'You'll have to ask them.' He was a cult guy. He wasn't Jim Jones, but he

DAN HICKS

had all these people up in Sonoma County working on some farm or something—he'd have the men go out and work hard and toil, and I don't know what the women did all day. One time, Bill said, 'If anybody ever says anything about wife-swapping in our group it's not true, and they don't know what they're talking about.'

I was still living on Delmar Street when Bill and Mitzi left, so this was probably in the spring of 1968. Patti must've left before Bill and Mitzi, because there was another singer working with Mitzi for a while named Lucy. Juicy Lucy. She was as tall as Mitzi, so now we got two tall girls. This was right before I signed with Epic, and it was getting toward the end of the whole Bill/Mitzi thing. Lucy had been a topless piano player in North Beach, and Mitzi thought Lucy's moves onstage were cheapening the act. I didn't think that especially, but they wound up getting into an actual fight backstage at a club in North Beach.

This just happened to be the night that some people from Epic came to check us out, and they're back there fighting, hair pulling, screaming, and shoving between sets. I think the problem was that Lucy was just a lot sexier than skinny Mitzi was.

Juicy Lucy showed up at a gig a while ago in West Petersville, Idaho. All these people show up again eventually. 'Hi! I'm Juicy Lucy!'

♠

Jaime came back from jail in June of 1968 and re-joined the group, and he introduced me to a guitar player named Jon Weber. I liked Jon and I still like him. Low-key is the definition for that guy. His picture is in the dictionary, illustrating the term 'low-key.' He was a macrobiotic guy, and he was the first guy I heard say the words *yin* and *yang*. That was the deal with him.

Then, right around that time, I found Sid Page in Santa Rosa. I'd gone there to take my mother out for a drink on her birthday, and we went to this place, the El Rancho Hotel, where I'd worked as a busboy during high school. Sid was in the bar, playing pop standards with a little piano, drums, and bass, and I approached him and he came down and auditioned. So Sid Page joined the community.

When I met Sid he was married to a woman named Sandy, and he was making a living as a shoe salesman—kind of a straight-arrow type of guy. When he joined the band he grew his hair out, and Sandy turned out to be too straight for what we were doing, so she was gone. Once Sid had a taste of that San Francisco poontang, he never looked back—he just left that Santa Rosa white-bread shit behind and got himself a motorbike. You wouldn't have imagined it, his long blond hair flying in the breeze.

With Mitzi and Patti gone, we needed girl singers again. I found Sherry Snow, who'd been a singer around North Beach and was part of a folk duo called Blackburn & Snow with a guy named Jeff Blackburn. It often happened that I'd meet a girl singer and she'd have a friend who was a girl singer, and it was good to meet singers that way, because the two singers were already friends. Sherry had a friend named Tina Gancher who played some piano, but she wasn't the greatest singer, so Sherry more or less carried it.

When we started out we rehearsed every day. I was living on the houseboat in Sausalito, and we would rehearse at my place, sometimes even on the roof of the houseboat. The early rehearsals were always fun, because we all liked making the sound. We were serious about it and were digging it, and I especially thought we were really doing something worthwhile.

See, the thing that's kept me going is music. It's not like, wake up, put in eight hours, go to sleep, have a hobby, and find something fun to do on the weekend. There's none of that for me. I got a consistent thing I wanna do, a lifelong preoccupation, avocation, and motivation—there's that thread running through my life. It's not as if I grew up believing I was destined to leave my mark on the world, though, because I didn't know for sure about anything. I might've thought or wished or hoped that I was something different and special, but throughout my childhood I felt like just another middle-class Joe. There were the great, famous people who did things, and then there were the Joes, and I was just another Joe. I had one thing going, being a drummer, but I was just an average Joe drummer. Then, when I was in The Charlatans, I was a little more than an average Joe drummer. I was a drummer in a known hippie band on the San Francisco psychedelic scene. I was more than just 'Joe Schmo: drummer.' Then, with the guitar and the singing and writing, I started getting little solo gigs by myself and getting my name in the paper, and I was more than a Joe Schmo drummer in a hippie band. I wanted to get these tunes together and go in front of people and play them and that's what I was doing. It was good.

We didn't read music when we were learning new songs. It was kind of like, 'Here's how the song goes,' and everybody joined in. The arrangements were always arrived at sort of collaboratively—maybe less so now—but what I'd do is lay out the skeleton or the outline of what's gonna happen, paying special attention to *when* things are gonna happen: when the girls sing with me, when they sing by themselves, when we have instrumental breaks, and when we have fills. As far as the vocals, it's always been that the girls think of their own vocal harmony.

The songwriting really kicked in then, too, because I finally had a vehicle for the songs. Songs like 'Evening Breeze' and 'Milk Shakin' Mama'—none of these songs were written until I got the girls in there. Most of the songs I wrote during that period ended up on the first album, which was all my songs. I don't work that way anymore—I cover other people's songs now, but always with my arrangements.

We had a reel-to-reel back then, and we'd record the rehearsals and listen to see how we sounded. I don't do that much now, but in those early days that was really fun. I was really digging that it was happening. I had confidence in the band and thought the sound was unique, and as far as my own ability, I guess I figured I was good enough to get onstage. I could hear the thing coming alive, and I thought I had something pretty special.

Then we got that good review in the *Chronicle* from Ralph Gleason, and that was kind of a turning point. It wasn't like that's when I decided to do The Hot Licks full-time, but it helped. I was still with The Charlatans when that review came out, and one of them said to me, 'What are you doing with us?' It was right around then that my mom changed her mind about me, too. She thought I was kind of a beatnik hippie, and was always saying to me, 'What are you doing?' Then I started getting my name in the paper, and she became Dan Hicks's mother, and she dug that.

DAN HICKS

♠

So we got signed to Epic and went into the studio and made *Original Recordings* with Jaime, Tina, Sherry, Sid, and Jon Weber—Jon played all the leads on *Original Recordings*, but he was only on that one album. As for the producer, Bob Johnston was a good ol' boy from Texas, and Epic's thinking was that he would be the right fit for us. He'd just been recording Bob Dylan and Johnny Cash, so his legend thing was happening then, and we were pretty excited. He kind of mistreated us, though. He shows up and says, 'It's so damn loose but it's so damn tight!' and turns out to be the kind of producer who says, 'I'll just let you play.' Not a whole bunch of guidance.

When we were in the studio, we almost did it live. We'd stand in a circle, just take it from the top and do the song all the way through until we had a good take. We didn't do much of that 'now we'll put the vocals on' kind of thing.

We recorded all the songs in LA, at Columbia Studios, near all the TV studios on Melrose Avenue, and we stayed at the Hollywood Center Motel, a place near Highland that had a pool and these cool, old-time bungalows set back from the street a little bit. I have 8mm film of this. I always liked LA in the early days.

Bob Johnston took the tapes back to Nashville, and then he sent us a mix of the sessions. Because he mixed it by himself, he left in mistakes he didn't know were mistakes, but we could all hear them. It was sloppy, he put echo on everything—it was a mess.

I was more or less my own manager then, so I called him and said I wanted to remix the record, and he said, 'Fine.' So we booked some studio time in San Francisco and the tapes were sent there, but when

96

97

PREVIOUS PAGE Justin Green comic published in *Pulse* magazine about the time Dan and The Hot Licks opened for Steppenwolf at the Cleveland Auditorium to a less than receptive audience.

LEFT AND ABOVE Dan with an early iteration of The Hot Licks on the porch of his houseboat in Sausalito, California, 1969. *Left to right*: Maryann Price, Sid Page, Nicolee Dukes, John Girton, Jaime Leopold, and Dan.

I SCARE MYSELF

Dan, David LaFlamme, and Bill Douglass in Golden Gate Park, 1968.

101

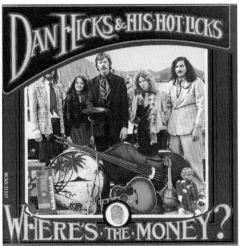

OPPOSITE 'Rare shot
of Jimmy the Talkin'
Dummy'—D.H. *Left to right*:
Jaime Leopold, Sherry Snow,
Dan, Tina Gancher, Sid Page,
Jon Weber. THIS PAGE Covers for
the three albums released by
the classic Hot Licks lineup—
Where's The Money?, *Striking
It Rich*, and *Last Train To
Hicksville*—and Dan's first solo
release, *It Happened One Bite*.

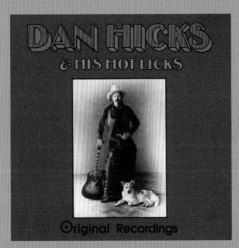

DAN HICKS
& HIS HOT LICKS

Original Recordings

OPPOSITE Dan with his dog, Fetch, in an outtake from the photo session for the cover of the first Hot Licks album, *Original Recordings*. **LEFT** The LP cover, as designed by George Hunter. **BELOW** Dan on episode three of *The Flip Wilson Show*, 1972, with Wilson and Melba Moore.

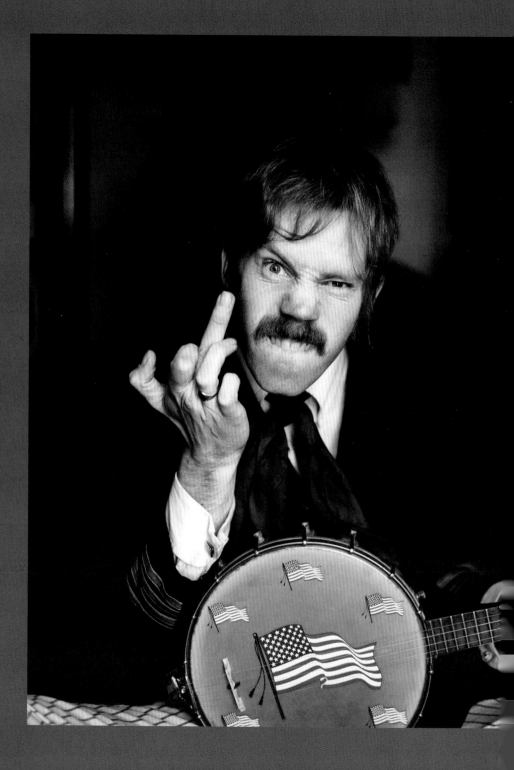

LEFT Dan in a mellow mood, c. 1968. **ABOVE** Dan with Candi Storniola during the same photo session.

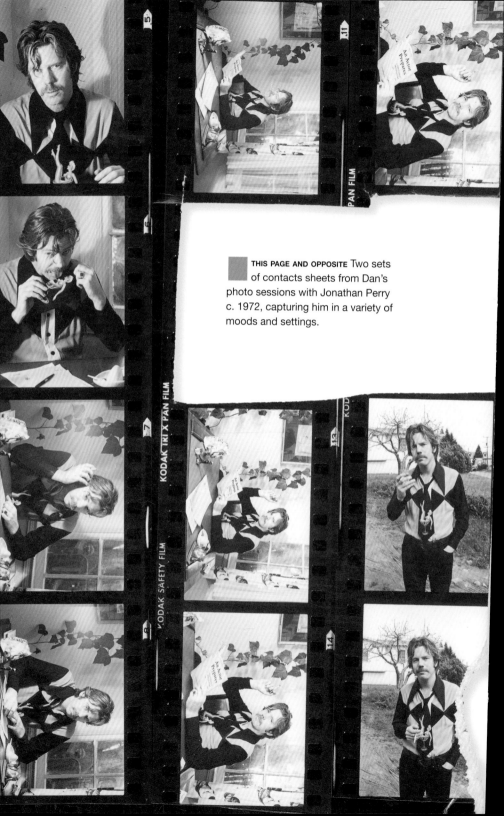

THIS PAGE AND OPPOSITE Two sets of contacts sheets from Dan's photo sessions with Jonathan Perry c. 1972, capturing him in a variety of moods and settings.

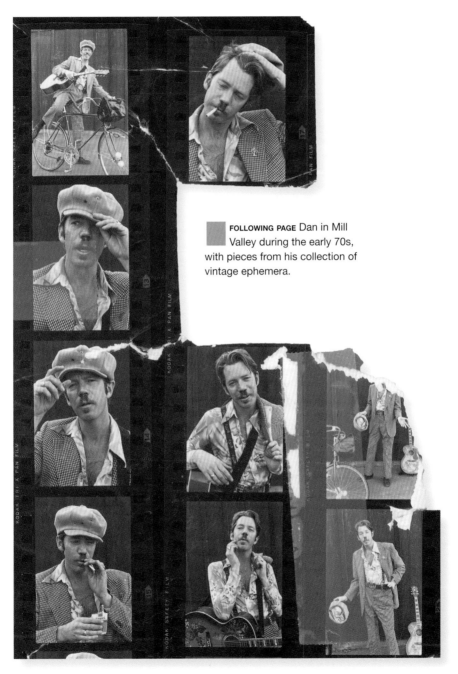

FOLLOWING PAGE Dan in Mill Valley during the early 70s, with pieces from his collection of vintage ephemera.

Jon Weber and I went to the studio to work on them, Bob Johnston didn't show up. We were told that he was stuck in Nashville with Bob Dylan, or some kind of name, so Jon and me and an engineer mixed it. It was OK, but it wasn't the greatest, because working in the studio was somewhat new for us. We worked with what we had, though, and Bob Johnston wasn't there, that's for sure. I was kind of happy with the record then, but today it sounds sort of lo-fi to me.

To finish the Bob Johnston story: one Saturday morning, Columbia/Epic was having a big convention at the Century Plaza Hotel to present their 'new product.' There were gonna be visuals and sound-bites, and some artists would perform for seven minutes, then on to the next artist. We were supposed to be part of the presentation, so I gave a bunch of visual material to somebody from Epic.

For some reason we weren't supposed to actually attend this thing—salesmen only or something like that—so Jaime, me, Jon, and maybe Sid snuck in and watched this presentation. So they go from one artist to the next, then suddenly the program is over, and we hadn't been presented. Where were we? It came back to me through the grapevine that they thought our music wouldn't stand up next to all the rock'n'roll, so they didn't show it. Anyhow, I see Bob Johnston in the hallway after this thing, and I want some answers. I wasn't loud or mad or anything, I just wanted to know what happened. Bob said, 'Let me find out about this,' then he walked away, and I never saw him again.

The record came out, but Epic didn't put us on the road. We played LA, San Francisco, and a few other places, and that was it, so we didn't really tour much at all. Jon Weber left after *Original*

DAN HICKS

Recordings, and Sherry ended up doing a similar kind of 'I want to sing for God' thing. She changed her name to Halima Collingsworth and left the band to pursue whatever religion it was that she was involved with. Her very words to me were, 'I want to sing for God.' I'm still in touch with her—she lives somewhere up near Crescent City. Most of my people go north after they leave. Jaime lives in Portland, Naomi's up there, and Girton's up there, too.

When Sherry left it was a good excuse to drop Tina, so at that point I needed some singers again. I had friends who worked at KSAN and KMPX, two Bay Area radio stations, so they announced to their listeners that I was looking for girl singers, and I got a lot of calls. Girls who wanted to audition would come to my houseboat, we'd sing some songs together, I'd tape it, then I'd listen to the tape. *What do we sound like together? Does it sound good?*

It wasn't that important that the girls be sexy. I always go for the sound, and any visuals are extra, so mostly they just had to be women. I did want the band to have a certain appearance, though, and I would have ideas for what they'd wear onstage, and might've bought something for them now and then—a little top or something. I still do that. There was only one black girl who auditioned, which is surprising. I guess I just put out this white vibe, because the band always ended up all-white.

I had open auditions like that twice, and the first time around, Maryann Price showed up. Maryann Stone was her original name, and she was from Baltimore. She'd been married to a drummer named Brent Price, who was also a road manager guy for Si Zentner, a trombone player who was a late-50s big band kind of guy. Before

114

joining The Hot Licks, Maryann had been working in Las Vegas, singing jazz with Si. I think she had a great voice—she's probably the best girl singer I ever had in the band. She was a cool, positive person, very *digging it*, always gregarious, and when strangers came into the dressing room, Maryann was always the person they'd talk to.

Nicolee Dukes joined the band after that first round of open auditions, too. She worked at a bank or something and was a real straight-arrow girl. We never recorded with her, but she was on quite a few gigs.

♠

We started recording a second record for Epic with Sid, John, Jaime, Maryanne, and Nicolee. This guy named Terry Wilson, who was a friend of Jaime's from the Electric Orkustra, might've been on those sessions, too, because he was in the promo pictures. We did these sessions in the Bay Area, but somehow that whole thing didn't get finished. I don't remember exactly what happened with Epic, but the upshot was that it was OK for us to find a new label, and we wanted to get off Epic. Nicolee started getting a weird attitude going right around then. I don't know what it was, but one time we were rehearsing and she was sitting there jingling her car keys, so I told her, 'If you want to go so bad, why don't you leave now?' And she did.

After Nicolee left I did a second round of open auditions, and that's how I found Naomi Eisenberg. She told me she'd auditioned for me before—I didn't remember her, but I guess she didn't pass the test the first time. Naomi went to Charles Evans High School in New York, which I think was all-black and had a lot of juvies, so she's got some of that in her—she was a streetwise New Yorker and a hippie chick. She wasn't a jazz singer like Maryann Price is a jazz singer, but she had a nice, strong voice, and they got along. I never sensed any kind of problem between them.

Naomi also played violin by ear, so she plays a little violin with Sid on songs like 'Is This My Happy Home?' You can hear her on *Where's The Money?* quite a bit. I think she was making a living as a topless dancer when she joined my band. She was in this thing called Dancing Food & Entertainment, and another group called The Dadas, but none of that stuff was going anywhere compared with hooking up with a swift cat like me.

We made a new demo with this lineup and went to the offices of some labels in LA, and they played the demo while we sat there, which was awful. I wasn't discouraged, though, because I definitely wanted to do this Hot Licks thing. It's not like we were hot shit yet, but we were getting there, and there were a few labels we could've signed with. We picked Blue Thumb because we thought they were pretty hip, and we just liked them.

Blue Thumb was owned by Don Graham, Bob Krasnow, and Tommy LiPuma, and Tommy understood the music. He was producing The Crusaders and George Benson during that period, and he was a good guy to be in the studio with. He'd point out things that weren't right, but he didn't try to redo it; he just kind of let you play the thing.

We decided to do a live album and recorded at the Troubadour to get *Where's The Money?* Even though it's a live album, I think it's one of the best things we did. We recorded for five nights and took the best takes of each song—we ended up taking quite a few songs from one particular night, I think it was Friday.

There's hardly any percussion on *Where's The Money?*, and there's no lead guitar, either, because Jon Weber had left. Tommy plays the tenor sax, and he can keep a beat, so Tommy and I overdubbed a little percussion, and I put congas on one of the songs.

I think 'Innocent Bystander' is the best thing on the album—that's a really good recording. A lot of these songs sound really good to me now, just tasty, the playing, and the mix, and the sound. Hearing it makes me appreciative of those people.

After we finished *Where's The Money?*, I thought it would be good to add a guitar player. The guy who owned the Red Dog, Mark Unobsky, was living in Mill Valley then, and he introduced me to John Girton, who was teaching guitar at the Prune Music store at the time. He was a guitar picker and he liked the blues. So John came over, and we liked each other, and I liked his picking—he was a great player, really good, and probably still is. So we got John in there. Then we got this lady manager named Gretchen Sherman, who'd worked for Bill Graham, and she went with us on our first tour in 1971. Gretchen was good for us and she was good for me. She died a couple of years ago. I hadn't spoken to her in a long time and I heard she was ill with cancer, so I called her. Steven Pilster was there on that first tour, too—he started as a roadie—and there was another guy we all liked who was mostly in charge of equipment.

That was the longest tour I've ever done. It lasted five or six weeks, and it's the only tour that isn't a blur. We played a lot of places and did lots of new things. We were on national TV shows and did some local television shows, too. We played a club in the Village for a week, and played out on the Jersey Shore—we actually played on the boardwalk in a big auditorium that's probably still standing there. We played some colleges in the northeast, and I remember staying at Maryann's house in New England and playing Scrabble all night. We headlined at the smaller places, and we opened for Elton John on a few dates.

We also opened a show in Cleveland, Ohio, for Steppenwolf, and the audience threw stuff at us. They wouldn't let us play, so we finally just left the stage, and that was the only time that ever happened. There were times when we were really just in the wrong place, and it's hard to know what the audiences thought of what we were doing. When the band was brand new, we were on a bill with Ten Years After at the Fillmore, and it was still the days when you couldn't get the right acoustics or get the room quiet. It was a joke.

We were touring in a couple of station wagons, so it was kind of grueling, but it was OK because everything was new and I was glad that the music was being heard.

After we got back from the tour, Maryann, Naomi, Sid, Jaime, John Girton, and I started working on *Striking It Rich*, which came out in 1972. That was the first time Girton was in the studio with the band, and we recorded the album in LA, in a studio on Sunset Boulevard across the street from Crossroads of the World.

It didn't take long to make *Striking It Rich* because we did a lot of it live. We'd stand around in a circle and do the songs. Tommy was with us again, and he had a guy come in named Nick De Caro who did string arrangements. We were pretty OK at that point, as far as

118

how the band was getting along, and I continued to be inspired by the fact that I could come up with a song, we could get together, and I could hear what I'd thought of come to life. That's definitely still a thing I love.

I was writing songs throughout this whole period, and was still getting ideas, no matter how good or bad they were. There were quite a few songs on the record that I'd had for a while, and some of them were from a first batch of songs I came up with when I finally got the girl singers. I wrote 'The Laughing Song' when I was living with Candi on Delmar, and I wrote 'O'Reilly At The Bar' way before the first album. 'You Got To Believe' had been around for a while, too. 'Walkin' One And Only' was a fairly new song, and 'Woe, The Luck,' which was originally called 'The Lucky Man,' had been around for a few years. During the dark years on Noriega, when I was actually living in a basement underneath a house, I got depressed enough that I could draw on feelings of depression to write songs, and 'Woe, The Luck' was one of those songs. I wasn't depressed when I wrote it, but I knew about depression.

'I Scare Myself' and 'Canned Music' had both been on the live album, and it was Tommy's idea that we do them again. The whole experience with Tommy was a big part of my Blue Thumb experience, and a lot of my good memories from that period involve him. I remember riding in his nice, fresh-smelling Mercedes coupe, and sometimes I'd sleep at his house.

We were still touring on-and-off throughout 1972, and I remember playing the Santa Monica Civic in May of that year. George Gobel's son was a fan of ours, and he came to the show and brought his dad along, and they came backstage. George Gobel ended up introducing us. He liked it onstage, too, and it was kind of hard to get him off.

♠

The relationships in the band were getting pretty bad by the time we went into the studio to make *Last Train To Hicksville*. Tommy was there again for *Last Train*, and he was able to rein things in, as he does. That was another one that was done pretty much live, and it was recorded in Sausalito at the Record Plant.

The girls weren't playing much percussion then—they play much more now—so I'd been using a drummer named Bob Scott at some gigs, and eventually he became a regular part of the band. My music is pretty exacting, and it's not like just anybody can play it—it's not like, 'we're gonna jam the blues.' The drums have to meld seamlessly into the music, and I always try to rehearse with a drummer, and sometimes I'll show them the part I want them to play. I don't know if it improved the music—I still go back and forth on the drummer question—but Bob was on that record, and Bob was good.

There are a couple of songs on *Last Train* that John and Maryann wrote together, and there are quite a few songs on that record that I don't do anymore. 'Lonely Madman' is too hard to learn to do live again. There've been songs that I spent a lot of time working up, then I never felt like playing them, and the band doesn't appreciate that after we've rehearsed a song a lot.

I started doing 'My Old Timey Baby' long before I formed The Hot Licks, but I never do it anymore, and I don't do 'Cheaters Don't

Win,' either. I don't know where 'The Euphonious Whale' came from—it might've come from a cartoon, Tweetie Bird, or Sylvester, maybe. 'Cowboy's Dream #19' I've kept alive, because it's a good song to do onstage, and it has a different sound than lots of the other ones.

'Payday Blues' I do at every show. I don't know why, but that's one they still clamor for, maybe because it's a drinking song. ''Long Come A Viper' was one of the first songs I ever wrote, and we do that every show, too. I think I might've written that one in 1964, on the trip with Dick, although Dick and I didn't do that song. I did record it with The Charlatans, though, with me doing the vocals.

Tommy had been in LA for a long time as a producer, and he knew lots of well-known jazz guys, so he took the tapes down to LA and had Jimmy Rowles add piano to 'Sweetheart.' Tommy would pay these guys double scale, and they were always willing—you know, a gig's a gig.

Jimmy Rowles was part of Billie Holiday's generation. I've got one of her records called *Songs And Conversations* that has her talking, reminiscing some vignettes and rehearsing with someone, and the guy she's with is Jimmy Rowles. You hear his voice every now and then. '*Well, yeah, is that when it was?*' She's a little stoned—you can hear this in her voice—and I was kind of surprised her family allowed these recordings to be released. When she breaks into some songs, though, the singing's good.

♠

It wasn't like I suddenly decided I'd had enough of the band. It was a more gradual thing. We'd been doing it for about five years, and I'd never thought, *I have to do this forever*. I didn't want to face it anymore, and I didn't want to be a bandleader. It just felt like the writing was on the wall, and this band was on the way out.

The money thing had always been a problem. Probably on the advice of Steven Pilster, we decided we should invest some of the money we made into the band, and instead of taking the money we made at gigs and splitting it up afterwards—you know, get in line, here's what we made—we bought an expensive string bass and a monitor system. I think I still have some parts from the monitor system. It didn't take that much money to get by then, but no matter what happened with the band, we were kind of stuck at a certain financial level, so it's not like we were walking away from good money.

There were a lot of funny personalities in the band, and we were forced to be together all the time, and we started getting bitchy and not liking each other. There got to be a kind of democracy problem, too. The people in the group today know they're working for Dan— Dan put in all these years, and we know it's Dan's thing. Back then, the people in the group started saying 'we want this' and 'we want that,' and it got a little bit out of hand. People were claiming that certain things were their idea when it wasn't exactly true.

The most problematic person was John Girton. He was sort of bitter, and he figured that he was as much responsible for the success of The Hot Licks as I was. Right around that point we were on the cover of *Rolling Stone*, which was kind of ironic that it happened then, and he said something in the piece like, he put the *hot* in *Hot Licks*. He seemed to think he could carry the whole thing. Like, 'I could do that, get me on *The Johnny Carson Show*, I'm funny, I'll just sit there and kill everybody talking to Johnny.'

He was hung up about attention and money and had a way of sticking up for his own rights, like he should make so much money; the contracts should be fair to him; blah, blah, blah. He was right about all that, but the way he expressed it agitated me. Once I got a new little suitcase, and he said, 'Gee, I wish I had enough money so I could buy a nice little suitcase.' He also said something in *Rolling Stone* about me getting a new contract with Blue Thumb that came with an advance of $30,000, and that I broke up the band so I could keep it all.

That's not why I disbanded the band.

Right around the time the band was breaking up, John and Maryann went to Nevada to get married, and, 'Would you like to come?' It was all that kind of thing. Weirdness. What are they asking me for? Do they like me? What would I go for? I didn't go. I don't know how long the marriage lasted.

There was a lot of wild-west shit in this scene, too, like semi-violent things, and there were definitely times when I was kind of loose. One night we were playing a gig in Lawrence, Kansas, and they were lining up pitchers of beer on the stage for us to drink, and it was kind of a high stage. Suddenly an inebriated customer shows up at my side and says, 'You're not singin' for shit tonight,' and throws the contents of a pitcher of beer in my face. He starts to exit to the right to leave the stage so I put my guitar down, and he's about to jump off the stage, and I grabbed him and we both fell down to the floor below.

DAN HICKS

Drugs may've had something to do with all this, too. I don't know why drugs are so much a part of the music world, but I do know that a certain kind of personality is drawn to people doing the drinking and drugging, whereas other people are not. And, if you're a musician, you're gonna find yourself in an environment that reinforces that part of yourself, if you're the type of person drawn to people drugging and drinking.

Even back in The Charlatans, I remember playing some show, and afterwards everybody went over to some house and smoked angel dust. There was always stuff around, and if you happen to like the feelings these substances give you, you're probably gonna partake. People who *do* like those feelings tend to be people who don't like the feelings they have when they're straight, and this is particularly true when you work yourself to where you're abusing stuff. You don't like how you feel on a regular basis when you reach that point.

During The Hot Licks I just took whatever came our way. I remember being in an office after a show at the Armadillo World Headquarters in Texas, and some guy had a big buck knife with coke on the end, and he was putting it up to everybody's nose. That wasn't the first time I'd had it, of course. I don't know when the first time was, but I bought my share of coke. You get enough coke and you feel like God.

Some musicians think dope makes them play better. Marijuana, speed, opiates, booze—partake of some of this and you'll be a little tipsy, sped up, or smacked out, and there's a possibility that you will be aided. I'm speaking from experience here, because I used to think heroin opened up some things for me vocally, and that my range

124

improved because I was loaded. I don't know whether that was true, but I do know that now I can do everything I was able to do back then without using anything.

So hard drugs started floating around, and all of this was sort of dope and alcohol-fueled. I was feeling pretty uninhibited, and sometimes things would happen onstage that probably shouldn't have happened. I was a little out-there, and there was uncalled-for behavior. One time we were playing a club in Chicago called the Quiet Night and Naomi was doing a solo song, and I noticed that the people at the front table right near the edge of the stage weren't listening and were making noise. I had a coke with ice in it, and I threw the contents of the glass on these people and said something to them about not listening. Then I said, 'That's worth a replay,' and I grabbed another glass of something, but they threw a beer mug that hit me in the chest before I had a chance to throw that second drink at them. After the show I apologized to the owner of the club, and he said, 'It's not your job to police the crowd.' Let's just say I didn't always have a good attitude.

I guess you could say that the semi-official ending happened at a meeting we had in my living room, in Mill Valley, before this gig in Sacramento. We were all sitting there, and I said I didn't care if we played the gig in Sacramento or not, and that became the last gig, *per se*. Prior to this, we'd signed with some hot-shit Hollywood management company called BNB. It was Buck Henry, Mace Neufeld, and I can't remember who the other *B* was. They didn't manage The Hot Licks for long. Anyhow, one of their people, this guy named Elliott Abbott, was at that meeting, and I didn't think much of his abilities. Girton

125

could see that the band was ending, and he said I'd have to pay him four hundred bucks a week—which doesn't sound like much now, but it was then—or he wouldn't play the rest of the gigs the band already had booked. So I had to pay him this money, and to be fair I had to pay everybody else that money, too. The whole thing had pretty much fallen apart by then, even though it was right at that point that a few things started to happen for us.

I think Maryann and Jaime probably would've kept doing it because they liked the music and liked some of the people involved. Sid was the first to go, so the band went along without a violinist for a while. He got sick of me and thought I was an a-hole, so I assume that's why he left. It wasn't because Sly Stone wanted him, although he did end up with Sly and was in his band for a while. If you see pictures of that band from a certain period, Sid is the ofay guy from Santa Rosa with the long blond hair. I recently saw some kind of documentary thing about Sly & The Family Stone on TV, and there's goddamn Sid. He's up there with all these black people with his long blond hair, playing violin. He didn't take a solo.

Supposedly there were reasons to keep managing me after the band broke up, so BNB—mostly Mace Neufeld—were still my managers, or were trying to be. I wasn't a very good client. I tried doing some tunes with Tommy for another album on Warner Brothers, but not much came of that. I leveled off taking a bunch of gigs, even though Blue Thumb tried to talk me into not stopping. I remember telling them, 'You have W.C. Fields on your label'—and they did—'and he doesn't tour.'

It was all kind of one big dysfunctional blur. I was getting out of control, and it was getting into the period where all I cared about was having another drink. I should've had a little more governance of my behavior, and I regret the way I treated a few people. I think of Mace, for instance. I wrote him a crummy letter one time. We were with William Morris for a while, and some guy who worked there—Peter Golden, I think his name was—I remember being in his office and being an a-hole. Stuff like that. Sorry, Peter.

It probably sounds weird, but I might've been happy after the band broke up. Yeah, I think so. My mom left me some money, and then I signed with Warner Brothers and got an advance of $30,000. So there I was, sitting on this money, and I didn't have to find a gig every week. Looking back, I guess you could say I was being self-destructive, but at the time it felt kind of *con*structive. I was enjoying the freedom and a certain loose attitude, and it didn't feel destructive to be down at the bar at noon. It felt fun. I was digging this carefree character I was becoming, and there were women who came and went. But the drinking began to be a problem not too long after The Hot Licks broke up. The kamikaze years.

tunnel vision

THE AFTERMATH OF THE HOT
LICKS' DISBANDMENT, A TASTE FOR
SUBSTANCES, LIVIN' LOOSE ...

I SCARE MYSELF

Not long after The Hot Licks ended, this Ralph Bakshi thing came up. It was called *Hey Good Lookin'*, and it was a movie that was animated by Bakshi, and they wanted me to do music for it.

This was in 1974. It was a little bit farcical. Bakshi had some studio, maybe on Melrose, and it was like a cartoon factory with people in little rooms bent over drawing things. I met him and he had the characters for the movie figured out, and it was a dark humor thing, Brooklyn in the 50s or something. I started coming up with tunes for his characters, and he liked my lyrics, and he said to me, 'I've got to employ more of these kinds of words in my movie,' and I told him about Mezz Mezzrow's book *Really The Blues*. Mezz was this Jewish guy who joined the black culture of the Chicago jazz scene during the 30s and 40s. It's a cool story, and there's a lot of language in there. I told him to check it out.

The idea when I started was, I'm gonna do all the music, and there would be theme songs for the characters. I was also supposed to do background music, like if there was a scene with a jukebox, I'd do that music, too. That's how 'Garden In The Rain,' 'You Belong To Me,' and 'Cloud My Sunny Mood' came in. They were incidental music and were different from songs like 'Buggaloo Jones' that refer to characters in the movie. I like 'Cloud My Sunny Mood,' but I don't perform it anymore because I just don't want to.

Then there was stuff like a scene where a guy's combing his hair, and it's all instrumental, then when he's done combing his hair, the vocal starts—stuff like that. So they gave me this old guy, Milton, I think his name was, and he was an old 'put music to film' type of guy. There's a formula of tempo versus frames per second so you

129

can match things up, and it's a mathematical formula that's really complicated. We tried that a little bit, but I didn't pay too much attention to it.

I was in LA for about a month or less, and I stayed at the Tropicana Motel. I had a little set up in my room with a four-track machine, and I was making demos there and taking them in to Ralph, and that went along OK. I've stayed at the Tropicana quite a few times, and I remember being there a lot.

I met Tom Waits at the Tropicana while I was staying there. My story goes that I was in the lobby one time and he was there. I knew who he was, and I think I was surprised to find out he knew who I was. He pointed out that I'd dropped a hundred-dollar bill on the floor. That's my story and I'm sticking to it. Yeah, he was just kind of standing there while I was doing something at the desk and he said, 'You dropped some money on the floor Dan,' and I said, 'You know my name?'

There was a screening of Ralph's movie while it was still being made, and there were line drawings up on the screen, frozen, and you'd hear the dialogue between the characters, and it had a little bit of my music at that point. The screening was sometime in the afternoon with a bunch of muckety-mucks, and when the movie ended, nobody applauded.

I wasn't depressed about it, because it wasn't my project, but it must've been hard on Ralph. He was a character, probably still is— he's a New York guy. He was one of those people who had a little bed in his office, kind of a workaholic type, who would stay there all night. I think Ralph was a little unsure of his direction with that movie, and I also think some money ran out as far as him being able to finish it.

We recorded the music I'd written for the film maybe in 1975, and Tommy LiPuma was around. Tommy knows a lot of people, and he brought some musicians in—like, we tried the guitar player from The Tijuana Brass, Tony Paisano—but they just weren't capturing the sound. Guys tend to go ahead and play what they know in the way they usually play, and they weren't getting the flavor. There's a certain feel to my music, and it was more to the point for me to just get Girton, Maryann, and Sid, which is what we ended up doing.

So we finished those tracks, and they sat around for a while. Then, in 1976, I went into the Record Plant in Sausalito with a kind of jazz standards group. We put some stuff on tape just because Warners had booked the time, and I was supposed to record whatever I wanted. Tommy LiPuma was supposed to show up, and he didn't, so I made a stab at doing some standards—you know, *name a song and we're gonna do it.* I didn't have any lyrics with me, but I thought I was such a God's gift that I could just ad-lib lyrics and it would be fine.

There's only one song from that session that I kind of like. It's called 'Lulu's Back In Town,' and it's got some really nice picking—I think it's John Girton and me both playing guitar. Mostly, though, I was pretty wasted. There's one point on the session where I think I even said 'fuck.' It's bad, but I thought I was in control of the situation, and that whatever I sang or said was good, because *I* was doing it.

So, those dysfunctional standards were in the can, and Warners had them. Now it's 1978, and *Hey Good Lookin'* still isn't done, and we don't know if it's ever gonna come out, and Warners decides they want to put out the music I'd done for the movie anyway. So I turned the recordings into kind of a takeoff of the movie *It Happened One Night*, and I called the album *It Happened One Bite*. I drew some art for the cover and wrote some liner notes, and they released it.

When the film came out four years later, it didn't have any of my music in it—it had a bunch of other music, more rock'n'roll type stuff. All the live action was cut out of the final version of the movie, too, except for The Lockers, and I kind of liked them. The Lockers were Toni Basil's dance team, and I liked that hit song she had, 'Oh Mickey,' too. It seemed like The Lockers were one of the only dance teams around in that period, and they were in a kind of *West Side Story* scene in Bakshi's film. The Lockers were on one side of the screen facing cartoon characters on the other side of the screen, and The Lockers had been rotoscoped, so they were very smooth-looking cartoons. So, yeah, the movie finally came out in 1982.

Meanwhile, Warners still had those recordings from the Record Plant, and in 2001 Rhino rereleased *It Happened One Bite* and added on those standards. It was music, it was me playing, so they just added them on. If anybody listens to them, I hope they don't listen too carefully. I was drinking on those sessions, and I'm glad I don't hear about those tracks too much.

♠

During that period in the mid 70s, I thought maybe I'd be a writer. I'd sit, sometimes in bars, and write out stuff on paper, just short things that were the beginnings of something. But by the early 80s, the bar thing kind of took over, and I wasn't doing too much but hanging out. I was in Mill Valley, and there were a few different bars, and there was definitely a cast of characters that frequented them. We got the Sweetwater, which is a little more uptown, and it's got entertainment and is known around the country. A few blocks away was the Brothers Bar, which was a whole step way down, and then we had a place called the 2AM Club. The lowest clientele of all was at the Fireside. And of course there was there was the Old Mill Tavern, where you could find me.

I don't know what my girlfriend status was at the time, but Clare Wasserman came along around 1976. For a long time I considered Clare a woman of mystery—she didn't reveal much and was kind of an enigma to me. She wasn't a real drinker, but she would show up at the bar and be hanging around. I liked her from the start, but it was a gradual thing, and there were other chicks along the way. When we first met she was kind of scared of me, because I was one of these unpredictable guys. She was a little gun-shy, so it wasn't an automatic thing with us.

Clare was born in San Francisco, and her dad was an international lawyer. They lived in Japan for a while when she was growing up, and she has a brother who's five years younger. Like a lot of people, she had trouble with her parents when she was growing up, and she dropped out of high school maybe when she was a junior. She wasn't a druggie or a hippie—she was eleven years old in 1965 when The Charlatans got together, so she was too young for the hippie thing. She just quit high school because she didn't want to go anymore.

I don't know how she got started, but when she was around

seventeen she started producing shows. She was real young, and Bill Graham was her mentor, and she started doing shows in places like women's prisons—she'd say, 'Yeah, I brought in The Paul Butterfield Blues Band.' When she was around nineteen, she met this Rob Wasserman guy, who's a bass player, and they got married, then a year later she had her daughter, Sara. Rob Wasserman played with me at one point, so that's got to be how I met Clare. Their marriage didn't last long, and fairly early in the game they became independent of each other.

Anyhow, during that whole time, like from 1975 to 1985, I still always had things going with music, but there was quite a bit of dope—opiates, cocaine, boozing, and arrests. I got arrested a few times for drunk-driving and various other things. I can't really measure the time, but I remember being in Mexico on July 4 and the bars were closed that day for some strange reason, and I was thinking, *God, everybody's celebrating back in the US, and I can't even get a drink.*

During that period I met this guy named Patrick at a gig. He was from France and was one of these guys who'll talk to musicians—you know the type—and I liked this guy. He was a furniture importer and a drinker I was hanging out with, and he had a wife named Carolyn who I liked. She had a twin sister who I also liked—two blondes—and I ended up with both of them. This guy had gone back to France for fucking ever—he might as well have been living there, or as good as dead—so it was time for me to move on in.

Anyhow, I'm thinking of this particular time when Patrick had a Chevy van, and he and his wife and me and his little kid started traveling around. The kid was around five. We were in the car and we picked up another French guy in Santa Cruz, and we just kept going south, and then stopped in Encinitas. And that's how I ended up in Mexico on the fourth of July.

There were times when I'd just decide that me and a couple of people were gonna fly somewhere spontaneously. Like, maybe we're in the car heading for the city ... no! Let's go to the airport instead! There was one time I did that in the late 70s, and the security person at the airport found a switchblade in my pocket. See, these kinds of things were like props to me. I might have a switchblade I got in Mexico for fun, and I might've put it in my pocket, but I'm not a guy who carries a switchblade. It might as well have been a flashlight. They took it from me but they didn't come down on me about it. I got away with a lot.

Drinking could make me volatile, and sometimes I'd get so pissed off that I'd jump out of the car, wherever I was, regardless of whose car it was. I'd hitchhike, whatever it took, to get home. Just so pissed. 'Let me out here!'

I got hauled in for drunk-walking in North Beach, outside the legendary restaurant Enrico's. They had an outdoor café in the front with little round tables, and there I was, and somebody came up to me and said, 'Can I write you a poem for a dollar?' So I went off on this person, maybe it was a girl, and I made her cry, and that's when the cops came up. That kind of thing happened occasionally.

One time I got hit by a Hells Angel. I was playing the Keystone Corner, a famous jazz joint in North Beach, and I said something derogatory to the crowd and I didn't know there were Hells Angels in there. During intermission I went to the bar and got a beer, and a guy says to me, 'You're kind of a wise guy, aren't you?' I started to say, 'I don't really think of myself that way,' but the guy hauls off and punches me in the face before I could answer him. I didn't go down—I may've even kept hold of my beer. I soon figured out that he was a Hells Angel, because he had the colors on, and there were these other Hells Angels there all of a sudden, watching this thing go down.

I said to the owner, 'You should ask these guys to leave,' and he said, 'I think you better sit down and be cool,' so I went in the dressing room, and then I left. I didn't go back up and finish the show because I felt that people were behaving in an improper way. I was indignant!

The next day I called the owner and told him, 'You and your friends can shove it up your ass,' and he said, 'You come over here and say that.' Then I started getting scared, and for a week I was watching my back, like every person behind me was possibly a Hells Angel. I'm a big 'fraidy-cat when it comes down to it.

They banned me from a radio station in LA because of a crack I made about the station when I was there to be on the air, and another time somebody told me they heard my name mentioned on the radio during that period, and the radio guy said, 'If I see him coming, I cross the street.' I had a rep.

I have reviews of some of the shows I did during my solo career after The Hot Licks, and the reviews are about my behavior rather than music. One time I was playing a club in this small town on Long Island—maybe it was Roslyn—that was owned by a guy named Eppie. It was very snowy and cold, and I had a solo gig for a couple of nights. A manager/booker named Mike Oster went with me, and we flew there and got in late at night. I think I may've stayed up all night, then I started hitting these bars, and the gig was coming, and I was a solo. I'd been drinking all day and I got up onstage and sang two or three songs, then I didn't want to keep going. So I left the stage and went into the dressing room, and some big bouncer guy is there, and I was pacing around the room telling him I was gonna punch him. They canceled the next night. Then, somehow me and this Mike guy went into New York City, and I started insulting everybody there. I took on the whole city! I was onstage in some after-hours club, and I was making derogatory remarks about some of the people in the crowd, like, 'Your lives amount to nothing.' I don't know what I said, but I said something.

Where do I get this stuff? If you're a naturally pissed-off person, you don't have to have 'things' to be mad about. It's in your blood. Anyhow, it was very bad, and the next night I went back to the place sober and I played for free. That onstage hostility is something that just doesn't happen anymore. It would take quite a bit for me to get really bugged.

I have a copy of the review of a show I did at a club called the Catalyst in Santa Cruz in 1976, and the headline is, 'Dan Hicks Bombs Out.' We got to Santa Cruz the night before the show, and I spent the day of the gig going to different bars, so I'd been on my own, traipsing around drinking, and getting more loaded. I remember lying on my back onstage, then running into what I thought was the office of the manager of the place and saying, 'I'm not gonna play until I get my money!' The morning after I did stuff like this, I didn't feel ashamed. I'd just think, *well, that was fucked-up*. It might've been

137

far in the back of my mind that I was an asshole, but I mostly didn't think about it.

In Hawaii, I got punched and thrown down some stairs in two different episodes. This was around 1978, and this friend of mine, Turtle VanDeMarr, and I went to Hawaii to play for three or four nights at a place called the Blue something. We were both drinkers, and we had some pretty good weed, too, and I was digging the weed. Then the weed ran out, so I drank a little more than I needed to, or maybe I was withdrawing from the weed—I don't know. So I was up onstage and was irritated by some people and I may've said something to them, then I took the mic stands and pushed them onto a table, which means the mics went, too.

I went to the bar and a jock type guy, maybe not the sharpest pencil in the drawer, who was a silent partner in the club, said something about not digging what I just did, and he hit me in the mouth. He broke one of my teeth—it was just hanging there—and I think I went down.

Turtle and I were staying in a place that was within walking distance of the club, and I was upset, and I walked back there and caused a little damage to the room, because I was so fucked-up— maybe I ripped a picture off the wall. Generally speaking, I'm not from that school of hotel-room wrecking, although I've got some history of destroying property. Then Turtle and me had to find a hospital, which was a surreal adventure. Turtle was driving, and we headed off into the hinterland and found some all-night emergency room where they put me back together with a little bit of wire, and gave me some codeine. Turtle had had enough of this by then, and he flew home the next day, but I stayed there and went to Honolulu. When I finally got home, I went to a dentist. It was fucked-up.

Another time I went to Honolulu on my own, to the same town, Lahaina, and I was smoking this strong weed that just put me somewhere else. I'd put together this little band of guys from Lahaina, and we were playing this gig and I started mouthing off onstage. It got out of hand, and then I looked around and saw that I was the only one onstage. All the other musicians left.

I was still getting nuts, and I was up all night, wandering around the town. I saw this hippie guy along the way, and on the main street we passed these two doors that opened onto a stairway, and I said, 'Let's go into this place.' The doors weren't open, but I pulled them real hard and broke them open, and we went up the stairs, and there was this night crew cleaning up the place—and it was the club I'd played the night before. These cleaning guys didn't know what had happened the previous night, so I went up on the stage where there were some drums and a piano, and me and the hippie guy started playing. It was a crazy man's idea of fun, and I was just seeing how much I could get away with, I guess. Then a guy shows up who'd been there the night before, and he said, 'You're not supposed to be in here,' and he pushed me down the stairs. Or he went down the stairs real fast, dragging me along.

Back in Mill Valley, my bar life continued. This place, the Sweetwater, started having movie nights every Wednesday, and Clare and her friend were organizing them. One night they were gonna show *Revolution*, and Clare and I were on the outs then. She didn't like me. I think I'd been banned from the Sweetwater—that would happen sometimes, and there'd be like only one place left in town that I could go to until a certain time period passed.

So I'm down the road, drinking at the Brothers, and this event is happening, and I'm thinking, *I'm IN this movie and they won't let me in there?* So I go to a pay phone and call Jeannie Patterson, who owns the Sweetwater, and I tell her I'm coming down there and I'm gonna wreck the place.

I roll in there and the film is on and a bunch of people are watching, and I went and stood in front of the screen and told everybody what I thought of them. Then I go into the men's room and I start tearing down the stuff on the walls. When I left the men's room I see these cops are coming toward me, so I immediately went down the back stairs to the outside, and there are some more cops. I put up my dukes and was acting like I was gonna fight them, but I came to my senses real quick, and they arrested me. Even the cops— this one cop said to me, 'Why do you drink so much?'

♠

Around 1980, I started to think that maybe this lifestyle was a problem. They raised the rent on the place I was living, and there was a dude I knew in Mill Valley, sort of a lowlife, dark character named Jeff, and he said I could stay at his house because he had an extra room. So I put some stuff in storage and I moved in there, and that's when I started a steady diet of lowlife.

There was an old trailer parked out by Jeff's house, and some guy who was a friend of his lived in this abandoned trailer from time to time. I remember him telling us that one time he crawled in there, it was pitch black, and there was already another guy in there. Like, he says, 'Is somebody in here,' and a voice replies, 'Yes, there is.' Yeah, lowlife. Jeff had an outlaw quality to him, like he would commit crimes, and he cleaned houses to make money and would steal pills and stuff from people he worked for.

So I moved into a room in his house, and there was just a mattress on the floor, and I stayed there for two years. I was drinking in the morning and waiting for the liquor store to open up—there was no joy. I still had some money from record royalties, but I didn't have a car, and I was falling apart. I'd really given up everything, but I wouldn't let anybody help. I played less and less and I was never happy at that house, never liked it—it was creepy. And I was creepy.

One time Jeff came home all out of breath, and he told me he'd just stolen a van. He'd busted through the fence at some storage place, and he had this van parked somewhere near there. I didn't know what to believe with this guy, and I kind of didn't even want to get the details. Many years later, I got a letter from his mother telling me that he'd died in a car accident.

One night I came home and the fire department was there. He'd gone to sleep with a burning cigarette or some such shit, so the apartment was burned inside, and it looked even crummier than before. The windows were boarded up—it looked pretty bad. Jeff also hadn't shown up in court for two DUIs, and this is bad news. So one morning I got up at 6:00 am and went down to the liquor store and got a couple of six packs. I actually threw up on the way back, but I had this beer, and when I got home there was a sheriff standing at the door.

DAN HICKS

I've got to enter this place because it's where I live, but these sheriffs are standing there. They say, 'Have you seen Jeff?' and I said, 'Naw, I haven't seen him.'

I went inside and Jeff's in there hiding in the bedroom. Then bam! Somebody's knocking at the door, so I opened it, and Jeff darts out the back over the fence. It don't look so good, and the cops said, 'Were you just talking to somebody in here?' and I said, 'No, I was talking on the phone.' The guy's got me lying now, plus harboring a fugitive.

I didn't figure I was going to have to do this kind of thing when I moved in with this guy. Here I am, I've played Carnegie Hall and been on *Johnny Carson* and had all kinds of success, and I'm doing this shit?

I hated my life then. I drank because I was belligerent and angry, and I was belligerent and angry because I drank. I'd drink a lot and didn't do much else. There were times when I'd stay in bed all day, then get up at ten at night and walk to the bar in the dark. I must be strong, because it takes a strong person to be that self-destructive. If you can lay in bed all day and watch kiddie cartoons with a bunch of beer on the floor—you have to be strong to feel that shitty and survive.

From 1982 through 1985 it started getting pretty dark. After two years at Jeff's, I moved a couple of times—I've now changed paths, and I'm on my own. For a while I lived in a little hovel underneath a house in Mill Valley. It was the size of a small house trailer and I couldn't stand up straight in it because the ceiling was too low. I had to lean over to walk around. I was there for maybe a year and a half, and then I moved into an upstairs apartment closer to downtown.

I SCARE MYSELF

While I was living there it got to a point where I was being an insomniac and not sleeping for long periods of time, just getting a few hours of sleep in the afternoon. It was hell on earth, just a nightmare, and this went on for several months. I'm on the bed watching TV with tin foil for an antenna, and this was in the days when there was only one channel on all night, the movie channel, and I started really isolating myself. I stopped going out and started buying booze and staying by myself, and I wasn't talking to people very much.

Sometime in 1985, I finally crashed and burned. Clare came over after something she'd gone to, and I guess maybe I'd fallen down. I was bleeding a little bit, I was foggy, groggy, everything—fucked-up. I hadn't seen Clare for a while, and she called a friend of ours, Bob Spinner, who was kind of a go-to guy, and between the two of them they decided to call the paramedics, and I was taken out to Marin General Hospital. I stayed there for a week, and during that time they had me on intravenous Valium, hooked up to one of those little stands that rolls around with you if you walk anywhere.

I stayed there for a week to dry out, and I was pretty out-there. I didn't have any DTs that time, although I think I had them one time in another episode. I was just weak and depressed. I remember some doctor coming in and seeing me and prescribing this and that, and at the end of this week I believe I went up to this rehab place in Calistoga called Duffy's. That could've been decided by that doctor and this friend of Clare's named Gregory who was in the program. He appeared, and he may've even driven me up there, but I stayed there only like three days.

I remember my first day there. They kind of shift you around a

143

little bit. First you're in one kind of room, maybe by yourself for a day, and then they shift you to another area, and then finally you're in with a bunch of people, men with cots or whatever they are.

Duffy's is pretty well known. I didn't like it and I didn't do anything they told me to do. I slept, I wouldn't go to the meetings, I wouldn't cooperate, then I got on a bus and came back and immediately picked up the drinking lifestyle again. I got fucked-up all over again, and a month later I ended up with the paramedics again.

I don't know who called them that second time, but it was probably Clare, because she was pretty involved. I spent some more time in Marin General, then I went back to Duffy's, but this time I did everything they said to do. I could've still been angry and resisting it, but also I was going along with it and cooperating. It could've been both at once.

While I'm there, a fellow I know from Santa Rosa named Tom Candrian, who was in the program, visited me and said, 'This is not doing you any good.' He thought being at Duffy's wasn't enough for me, so we got this other place. I went over to Azure Acres, and I think he was right, because there was more of a regimen there, more of a get up at a certain hour, more of whatever it was—there was more of that. He went to my apartment and got some clothes and brought them to me, and it was really a help.

♠

I was at Azure Acres for twenty-eight days, but not drinking didn't change my emotional abyss. That didn't do anything to it. From there I went to this residents' place, Marin Services for Men, and I was there for about a year and a half. For me it was a halfway place between Azure Acres and getting back into the real world and living on my own somewhere. At that point I definitely didn't want to go back to the Mill Valley scene where I'd just bottomed out. I knew I couldn't do that.

The place itself was a three-story building in a residential area of San Rafael. It was cream-colored stucco, a big place with a bunch of little bedrooms. I don't know what the building was originally built for, but it had a dining room, a living room, and a garage by the street. The furniture? You didn't pay much attention to that. It wasn't run down. It was just like somebody said, 'Furnish the place.'

Marin Services was run by this woman who was ten or fifteen years older than me named Jennifer Wreden, and she was a tough-as-nails type. She was real strong, could swear like a sailor, and would really ream you out if she thought you were lying to her. A heavy-duty chick. She didn't live there—she lived in Novato—and there was an inmate or client or whatever who was the monitor head guy. But she would come in in the morning and run this thing all day. There'd be episodes where she'd have to get strong, and she could do it—there was no guy who could outdo her. It was impressive and she had the respect of everybody.

The first days there, you're kind of in the detox room. Even though you're sober and you've been that way for a month, you're still in this transition room with maybe three other guys. You're sleeping a lot and the other people in there are in the same condition you're in and they're just lying there, too. It was horrible. You know, *what have I done to myself? My god. Look at where I've gotten to here.*

DAN HICKS

I wasn't the guy who was on the cover of *Rolling Stone.* I was this guy lying there. There was no denying it. There you were. You feel like you're not experiencing what other people are feeling, and you have a box around your head, and you're miserable and sick, and you don't see any future, and you don't like yourself, and you're going through the motions of being awake. You doubt your future, and I doubted whether I'd ever resume my career. You doubt whether things can change. I felt stuck, like, *I know I'm gonna go down to the bar, I'm not makin' any progress.* It's hard to think you're gonna change, and I still struggle with that. I work a lot on change in myself now, and I don't know if I'm ever gonna get it.

There were fifteen guys in this place and everybody had a room, and a few people had roommates. We'd all eat together downstairs in the kitchen, and we had meetings in the living room. Some of the guys were there because they had the choice of being there or going to jail, so the place had a little bit of a prison vibe, and there were criminal-looking guys in there. There were all kinds of guys. Weird personality guys, alky guys, tough guys with tattoos, an Aryan guy, meth guys—all kinds of guys. There were a couple of weaker, wimpy guys, but there weren't many sensitive lost-artist types like me, and mostly it was kind of rough trade. It could be a little scary. There weren't many old guys. I was forty-three, and I think I was the oldest guy there. Most of the guys were like twenty on up.

I never made any real friends while I was there. At that point in my life I wasn't close to anybody. But I knew I needed to be there, and being surrounded by people was part of the recovery, so I just accepted it. The whole thing was a long, awful process. I was so under

146

it that I felt like I should be there. Everything I did, from the twenty-eight-day rehab place, Azure Acres, to everything that came after, was based on the twelve steps, which I embraced as best I could.

There was one TV in the living room, and sometimes the muscular, tattooed guys—especially this one guy—made it clear that whatever he wanted to watch is what we all watched. This guy was real strong and had a temper.

I only saw one physical altercation at a meeting. One guy had jumped from a building, and although he survived, he was all mangled up. He was one of the guys in my early detox room. A real ball of joy. Some guy at a meeting gestured toward him and said, 'The worst thing for me in sobriety is this guy over here,' and the guy ran over and did something to him. But mostly you never saw stuff like that.

There were little things you had to do. During the week, maybe you washed the windows in the living room or cleaned the bathrooms or whatever, and at a certain point you were supposed to get a job while you were still living in the house. So I went down to the State of California employment place, and the only thing I qualified for was picking weeds. I got a one-day job chopping poison oak on a slanted hill, and you had to chop this stuff and put it into bundles, and I was stricken with poison oak so badly that I had to go to a doctor, and it cost me more money than I made that day. Isn't that great? But Jennifer kind of let me slide, because I'd say to her, 'I got a job—I'm a songwriter.'

I'd been a heavy smoker since 1965, and when I first got to Jennifer's I was smoking a couple packs or more a day. I'd wake up, and before I got out of bed I'd light a cigarette. At that point I'd lost not my ability to play but my agility on the guitar, and I remember going down to the basement of the place where nobody could hear me and trying to play again. I was smoking so much, though, that I wanted to put down the guitar and have a smoke—that's how bad my smoking was. Then, when I woke up on my birthday there, on December 9, 1985, I quit smoking. I didn't smoke that day, and I've never smoked again.

You weren't restricted to the place, but there was a curfew. You could get a pass for the weekend, but you had to be back by eleven at night. My daily routine was I'd go to downtown San Rafael and sit around. Then I'd work my way back to the place, and then it would be time to eat. And then the meeting. So I just killed the days.

What kept me going? My heartbeat. What was I supposed to do? Scream bloody murder and run away and find a bar in Fresno and start drinking? It was kind of unbearable, but I didn't feel anything when I was killing the days. I just felt numb and accepted that this was me. I told Jennifer about this state of mind I was in and she told me about a doctor, so I went to this doctor and he gave me something to help my depression. It helped a little bit, but my state of mind kind of stayed the way it was.

I didn't play at all for a while, and then there was a period there where I had to sit with my guitar and kind of reacclimate, to teach my hands to start working again. My friend Turtle and I used to drink together, and we'd say that the hands go first when you drink too much. You can't play because your hands just aren't doing what you want them to do, and I experienced that.

I was a little nervous about playing in front of people, but I started performing again while I was still at the halfway house. I remember having my picture on the front page of the local paper when I was still in the halfway house, and that was kind of funny, me being a guy who's sitting in the loony bin.

I remember being in the halfway house and going to Texas to perform at Farm Aid in July of 1986, and playing with Asleep At The Wheel. It was kind of bizarre. I didn't quite feel like I was in the right place with those country & western people.

When I first started gigging, there were thoughts like, *OK, the gig's over, now where's something for me?* There would usually have been a drink. Most people didn't know what was going on with me, and they'd say, 'Hey Dan, buy you a drink?' But that happened less and less as time passed.

♠

Eventually enough time went by, and by 1987 I felt strong enough to go get myself a place. It was time for me to go back to Mill Valley. I was doing pretty good and had started gigging again. The Acoustic Warriors was the first group I put together after getting sober. I'd used that name at some point previously, but I'd dropped it, and then I started using it again. There were no girls in that band—it was just guys, and there was guitar, violin, and a bass, and I did that for quite a while.

I had this cool little bungalow after I left Jennifer's place, and I was going to AA meetings. I wasn't liking them much, but I felt better. I remember sitting in the sun outside of my house liking the days a little better.

DAN HICKS

By 1994 I was smoking pot again, and I was starting what turned out to be bad slip. I'd been smoking pot for about a year. I was playing a gig at the Fairmont Hotel, and they gave us a hotel room, so I stayed there one night, and then wound up staying for a week, using the room. Some other people had been there using the room, and I found half a joint and decided to take a puff on it, and that's what got me going.

Before the pot came along I'd stopped going to AA meetings—fuck that. I didn't like the meetings and I grew away from them. I'd been reluctant to talk in them and I didn't feel good. I finally found this meeting I go to now, and it helps. Before that, I was feeling these kind of inferior feelings and felt uncomfortable in meetings, and I don't feel those things in this meeting.

So, in 1994, I had the pot thing going, and, there was a week where I'd had some kind of problem with Clare. She was not pleased with me; I was trying to get a hold of her and it wasn't working too well. I had a rent-a-car then, and I decided to go over to the house of a longtime friend named Slim Chance and talk to him. This friend lived in LA, so I took off in the middle of the night in this rental car with some weed, and I was kind of nuts.

I drove down there and saw him in the morning, and I got a little hotel room while I was visiting him, and I talked him into going down to Mexico with me. We went to Tijuana, and I remember thinking about how the times I'd gone there before were kind of cool, and we'd had fun. But when we got there it was kind of nowhere. There were no white people and it was late at night, and a bunch of Mexicans were looking at us.

To get into Mexico you had to walk across the border then get a cab into downtown Tijuana, so we did all that stuff, then we turned around and went back to the border and walked back across. I was feeling really bad about this Clare thing, and Slim started getting upset because I think he'd lost his driver's license. Even in that short period of time he'd lost something there, and he was all bugged.

So we got to the car, which was parked by the bridge where you walk across into Mexico, and somebody had tried to break into the trunk while we were gone. We started heading north, and Slim is upset, and somewhere around San Juan Capistrano he stops the car and he's standing over by a tree, being upset.

When he got back in the car, I said, 'I want to go to a liquor store,' and that's where I bought the booze. I thought I was gonna be rough and tough and do all that stuff again, and I bought a bottle of Southern Comfort. I was sitting there in the car, and I was so miserable, and I asked myself, *what are the people in the program gonna think if I buy something to drink?* Then I thought, *well, if I don't tell anybody* … and I had this bottle, so I drank it, and then went to sleep where I was staying.

The next morning I felt like I could drink again. I woke up and thought I could drink like a regular person and have a drink or two, which is not what you're supposed to think.

After I got back to Mill Valley, I got busted for being drunk in public, and then I got busted for driving drunk in Larkspur. For some reason I didn't want to go back to my place, so I was staying in this guy's apartment who lived near this bar in Mill Valley—somehow I got to this apartment with some guy I didn't even know. He had something you snort, and I took it and started hyperventilating and reacted really bad. I couldn't breathe. Then I heard him make noises that meant he was leaving, and he said, 'See you later.'

I still don't know who that guy was. Maybe someday I'll run into him somewhere and he'll say, 'Hey man, remember when we had that toot?'

I crawled out to the living room and called an ambulance, and one of the paramedics who showed up had just seen me recently, because I'd gotten into so much trouble in just a few weeks. They made me walk down these stairs, and I kept saying, 'I can't breathe, I need air,' and they took me to the emergency room, and I said to myself, *what am I gonna do with myself?*

I know what I'm gonna do: I'm gonna quit all this stuff and go back to the recovery house.

So I called Jennifer at about six in the morning and went back to her place, and I stayed there for a year. Then I wanted to leave, not because anything bad happened—I just wanted to go back to Mill Valley. This guy named Guy Baldwin was running a residential place like Jennifer's in Mill Valley, and I remember sitting in the car outside his place with Clare, wanting this guy to show up, and feeling kind of desperate. I was nervous, and I really hoped he'd have a space. So he shows up: there he comes, getting out of his truck, and I go and talk to him and I got a room in the place.

Guy was a kind of businessman, and he played some piano, and I think he was a playboy in his day, you know; a swinging guy on the scene. He was a good guy. He was diplomatic and knowledgeable, and I could ask him about things. He died four or five years ago—

from melanoma, I think. He'd moved back to Santa Barbara, where he was from, and one day, after not being in touch for a long time, I called him up, and he was on his deathbed. Really, he had about a week to go. He said, 'I'm not usually taking calls, but for you Dan— I'll talk to you.' So I got to say goodbye.

♠

I was at Guy's in 1995. I remember the O.J. Simpson trial was on TV while I was there. At one point an older lady moved in, but it was a men's thing primarily, and Guy's was a more easygoing place with gentler, kinder people. It wasn't all tattooed guys who were trying to avoid jail time and liked to hassle each other. Guy's place was a regular tract house in the flatlands of Mill Valley with maybe five bedrooms, and I paid extra to have my own room. After I'd been there a while I got my own phone, and I started talking to people about gigs.

This was another period when I was not real happy. I don't care how much booze I didn't drink, I just didn't fuckin' feel good. It was mostly counting the days for me at Guy's. You can kill a goddamn day if you're good at it—there are ways to kill a day.

All through that period I could be counted on to go off on somebody. Mr. Nice Guy can turn on a dime and abuse somebody. That anger thing is still present but the really getting bugged is less frequent. I've always believed that if you're not sort of angry at everybody then you're not thinking, you're not living, you're not conscious. I'm paraphrasing somebody here, so don't credit me with this observation.

DAN HICKS

It took a long time to feel better, and it was gradual. I started going to a meeting in Sausalito with Guy, and that meeting helped. It was a small group, maybe fifteen people, and I felt better just being with people, and I kept going every night. A lot of the same people came, so you'd see them every night, and it had what I'd call a 'recovery-lite' thing. There was a good attitude there, and there was levity, and it was informal, and there's no pressure to share.

What I never liked was the pressure to share, to have somebody make me talk, and I still don't like it. As a matter of fact, there was the threat of that happening last night at the very meeting I'm talking about. The girl said, 'I could call on somebody,' and I felt shitty from that second on, because I don't like it. I like to sit there and get the message and not have that fuckin' feeling, because I am not automatically spontaneous with a lot of glib news for the people. I'm an infrequent sharer. That was a good thing about being at Guys, getting acquainted with that meeting, and I've been going ever since.

Your goal from the start is to be able to leave the recovery house and live on your own again, and you know that you're not gonna be in this place forever with the lady in the next room with her classical music coming through the wall, and the sounds of the other guys doing whatever it was they were doing. So, after about a year, I left Guy's. I got some stuff out of storage and moved into the place where I live now, and Clare moved in a few months later.

I'd lived alone for a long time, but I think I picked up on it OK. I think it was helpful because I started thinking of the other person, and I hadn't had to do that before. Well, I'll get two quarts of milk instead of one—you know, a little more consideration of your fellow man.

I SCARE MYSELF

I'd started doing a few shows while I was still at Guy's with different people backing me up, and I liked getting back to playing. It was scary to me to be back out in that world, though, and there was a period when I didn't want to do it. I was feeling really withdrawn and wasn't suited for getting up onstage and talking to people, being a personality and everything. But it was what I did, and I knew I was gonna end up getting back to doing music.

♠

There are lots of meetings in Marin County, day and night, and I go maybe three times a week. At just about every meeting, somebody says something about us being the lucky ones. I don't know why some people can end up staying sober and being in the program and others can't. Obviously there was a part of the people who quit the program that wanted to stop drinking, but it takes you. It's cunning, baffling, and powerful, as they say, and you can succumb to alcohol and hard drug abuse and end up drinking yourself to death. There are people I knew before I got in the program, and they ended up dying. They went out, as we call it, and they stayed out. I remember one guy who used to call me from hotels and talk crazy. I guess he was having booze delivered to the room, and he was very seriously gone. It was bad, it was awful. He died, that guy.

I hear a lot of people at meetings talk about their alcoholic parents and how they were afraid to go home because they didn't know how their dad was gonna be, but I never had any of that stuff. I never knew of anybody on either side of my family that had this problem, and never heard anything like, 'You know, your uncle Fred

155

was an alcoholic.' There was nothing like that. My mom had a little wine, my dad had a few beers, but I never saw either one of them drunk. It was never ever any kind of an issue in my immediate family.

When I told my story in front of a group for the first time, I remember saying that I felt like I was born with the destiny of being a substance abuser. I was born to get there, and I was that person from the get-go.

So yeah, I got sober, and I made my feeble attempt at making amends, but maybe the real deep things I don't have words for. There may still be a few things I haven't done, but I do it a lot day-to-day and don't like to keep things not right. If something happens, I get back to people. I talk to them about it. You got to.

♠

Feeling alone is part of this thing—you get very alone in alcoholism—but I don't feel alone anymore. I got Clare. Clare means a lot. We got married in 1997, up at Lake Tahoe.

I'd never felt strong enough about anybody to get married, but I knew Clare was the one for me. Sometime around 1996 she finally got officially divorced, and it was decided that we'd get married, and that the best way to go about this was to go up to Tahoe.

It wasn't like we were gonna go to the Elvis Chapel. We'd gone to the city and gotten wedding rings, so there we were with Reverend Stevenson, this little minister guy who was on staff somewhere up there, and we did the ceremony on the back deck of our rent-a-cottage. Then we went into Reno and had dinner, and when the waiter came over to take our order I debated whether to say, 'And my wife will have … .' It would've been the first time I ever said that. Then we went to Smokey Joe's Café, where they do a stage show of songs by Leiber and Stoller.

Clare still does a lot of shows and takes on different stuff—she's still quite capable. I think she likes the challenge and likes getting different people together and making certain kinds of music happen. She likes things to turn out well. Every year the Mill Valley Film Festival asks her to be part of things, and she gets asked be part of stuff like that a lot. I sit here when she's doing all this groundwork for this or that show, and it takes months, and she's on the phone—she's good at it. So yeah, I was cool with the marriage thing.

Over the years I was often on the outs with Clare, and that always affected me. Always. It was like a soul-sick downer thing in the back of my mind that I just had to live with and carry on anyway. When I look at her I wonder if I was ever really in love before her. Having a crush isn't the same as being in love because you're not thinking, *I like this person, but there's gonna be somebody else in ten years that I like a lot better*. I never thought that with Clare. She's the great love of my life.

on
music

GETTING INSIDE AND LISTENING
TO EVERYTHING

I SCARE MYSELF

Jazz makes me feel good in a certain way, and it also gives me something to think about. I'm not thinking that much when I listen to most rock. Maybe it's because jazz is more complex, if that's the word, but it appeals to a part of the brain that other kinds of music just don't reach. At least it appeals to people who *have* that part of the brain. Joe Six Pack, he's gonna like a rebel yell and turn up Lynyrd Skynyrd, and he's gonna stand up in the back of his pickup and can't wait to get to the big concert. It's a different beat. Jazz is more linear, and rock is more up and down and jagged.

So jazz is the kind of music I just naturally gravitate to, but lots of kinds of music went into the music I ended up playing. For instance, 'How Can I Miss You When You Won't Go Away?' is a country song, so I could be categorized as country in certain areas. Way back, early on, I thought about being a country singer, get that electric steel guitar and go electric, and just sing country tunes, but I decided not to do that.

When Zsa Zsa Gabor met Elvis, she supposedly said, 'Country music is for peasants, isn't it?' But there's some good country music. Any kind of music can be good, and any kind of music can be lame if it's done wrong. I've always appreciated black gospel, too, and even what they call white spirituals, Southern stuff, sort of mountain white spirituals. I'm not especially there with the theme that God will save us, but I like the music part of it. Maybe it comes from back when I was a Lutheran and had to sing these church songs, little hymns.

Dixieland has always been there for me, too, part of the jazz tapestry, if I may. There's a certain weaving that happens with Dixieland. The trumpets playing melody, and the trombone and the clarinet each have a role, and they're kind of weaving in and out, and then people take solos. The musicianship is usually pretty good with Dixieland, too, because you have to be kind of precise to play it.

When you're first learning how to play the guitar you play blues, because there's only three chords, and it's kind of easy compared with lots of other kinds of music. There's some blues in my stuff, too. You can define blues a couple of ways. There's the hardcore guitar blues, that's one thing. Then there's also anything that's just a twelve-bar blues tune with a blues feeling. I still do some blues—'Doodlin'' is a blues tune, for instance. It's not like, 'My woman done left me this morning, I got the empty bed blues.' It's not one of those tunes, but it still has a blues feeling.

All the standards—the stuff known as the Great American Songbook—have been a big love of mine ever since I started playing drums in Santa Rosa. I was playing dance music in little combos, what they call 'casuals,' one-nighters at the Elks Club or someplace, and standards is mostly what everybody played.

You might ask what makes a standard different from other kinds of songs? A standard has longevity, and it's flexible and it's open to interpretation. I have copies of *Billboard* magazine from the early 50s, and sometimes the same song would be in the charts at the same time performed by two different people. You can do that with a standard like 'Smoke Gets In Your Eyes.' There are corny songs that are standards, too. Somehow they pass the test of time, for whatever reason. Most standards are about love, too.

Romantic love is a subject people just naturally go to when they're writing songs. Maybe somebody is actually having some kind of love thing and they write about it, but that doesn't *have* to be happening. People have asked me where I got the idea for this or that song, and I say, 'It's just a fertile imagination, man.' There was no 'Milk Shakin' Mama.' You don't have to experience something to write about it.

I'm not currently feeling the need to write anything, and the drive to do that is something that comes and goes. Somebody was talking to me about writing songs recently, and I said, 'Man, I'm tired of rhyming—why don't you rhyme for a while?' I am writing though, because I write some of my own lyrics for the standards I've been doing. I'd say there are maybe a hundred standards I know well enough to perform, and I usually perform the ones I'm currently digging.

Sinatra could sing those songs, with Nelson Riddle and Billy May, and whoever backed him up. I don't know much about the early part of his career when he was a teen idol—he hadn't really come into his voice yet during those years. But when he got to his more mature, high, sensitive voice—yeah, he could sing those things, and he had a good sense of swing. He knew how to phrase a lyric, and that's important. You can sound pretty square if you don't phrase well. The players he worked with, and then he went on to become an actor—yeah, he could stretch out, and I gotta hand it to him: he was the man and was something to be reckoned with. He was like an entity.

There are different kinds of jazz. For instance, there's Django Reinhardt. I came upon him sometime around the tail end of The Charlatans. I don't know how I encountered his music, but I immediately liked the acoustic aspect—no drummer, swinging, and doing all the standards. Yeah, I think he was an influence. The violin is definitely part of that sound, too, and it's another lead instrument that takes solos and plays melodies.

Django never became big in America, maybe because America had plenty of its own small combos. He came over and played with Duke Ellington, so there was some recognition here, but maybe Django was too European and ethnic. I think people thought it was gypsy music, especially if you read anything about him. It's hard music to play, though, all that fancy finger work, and although there are lots of people playing it now, when I started there was just a handful, or less. Gypsy jazz is definitely a whole category now, though.

The one time I was in Paris, which was around 1976, I went to this place that was a Django bar. There were big pictures of him on the wall, and there were kids in the corner, like around twelve years old, playing Django music. Fats Waller is another player from back around that time who plays another kind of jazz I like. He's got that old-timey swing beat, good lyrics, and kind of a light approach that appeals to me.

♠

I was an average drummer and there was nothing spectacular going on, especially in the solo department, but I must've kept pretty good time, and that's an important part of playing drums. Sometimes you'll get a drummer who'll rush, and by the time you finish the song it's going faster than it was when it started, but this is something you can work on. You can get a metronome and improve your time. Paul Smith, who played bass with me for a long time, worked with a metronome for quite a while because he said he didn't want time to be something he didn't do well.

Keeping time is only part of what the drummer does. The drummer is also responding to what the other musicians are doing, especially when they're soloing, and they can add fills or accents, or do this thing on the bass drum called 'droppin' a bomb,' which is an accent on the bass drum. *Ka-boom*! They're just part of the swinging sound, part of the ensemble, and their style has to fit the style of the other players or it's not an ensemble. It's got to fit, and the drummer's got to be as good as the other guys.

I like this guy named Joe Morello, who was Dave Brubeck's drummer. He was influential. There's something called 'independence' that Joe Morello did a lot. You keep a steady thing going on the right cymbal with your right hand, then you play little fills with your left hand, things against the steady beat the right hand is keeping.

The drumming you heard in the psychedelic music of the 60s was rock'n'roll drumming, and it's pretty simple. It's a lot to keep up with, though, and you have to have some skill. I was involved in that music during the 60s, I was part of it, and I went to the dance halls even when I wasn't playing. I was out there dancing, and I liked a lot of that music, too. The Byrds, for instance—I loved their sound when they first came out. So yeah, I was involved with that music then. Part of what I liked about playing when I first started out was that I got to hear all this good music. I had a good seat.

My second musical love after jazz was acoustic folk music. The Jim Kweskin Jug Band came along, and they were the most funky. I liked the individuals in the band and the lifestyle they put out there, and the fact they were like a band, like Bob Wills, and I was immediately attracted to their songs. They had good taste in arrangements, and Kweskin also fingerpicked, which was cool, and various elements went into their music—they were jazzy. I used to think of bluegrass as sort of advanced folk music, because the musicianship in bluegrass is a little more demanding than what a solo folk singer has to come up with. A jug band is one more step up from bluegrass in terms of the musicianship it requires, and the vocals were good in the Kweskin band, too. Geoff and Maria Muldaur and Kweskin are all good singers.

I remember seeing them on *The Steve Allen Show* before Maria was in the band. They did a close-up of Fritz Richmond, and he had sandals on with no socks, which meant something at that point. It was kind of nowhere how they treated these guys. Steve Allen said, 'What do you call yourselves,' and Kweskin said, 'We call ourselves musicians.'

Fritz Richmond was wearing these little blue glasses and had an uncompromising kind of look and he said, 'People look at me and think I'm a freak, then when they see me play the jug they *know* I'm a freak.'

I got to know Geoff Muldaur at a certain point, and he was surprised by some of the stuff I knew about the Kweskin band. I said, 'Man, come on, I'm a fan.'

My approach to singing has changed over the years. When I started out, I could only do so much, and I used to kind of go off key, but I stay on pitch now, and I'm more agile. I can do more, and my range is bigger.

I SCARE MYSELF

I'm not a vibrato guy. In fact, I overemphasize *not* using vibrato because it gets out of hand and notes end up lasting longer than they're supposed to. I have a Sarah Vaughn record with so much vibrato, it's just so wide. She was a great singer, but I don't know what that vibrato thing was, if it was later in her career or what.

Anyhow, performing the jazz stuff the way I've been doing it for the last few years has helped with all that, and it's been freeing. I don't have the guitar when I do those gigs; I just stand there and sing, and I can think about just that. I'd like to do some singing in more of a jazz setting, too. I'm not saying I want a horn section or anything— maybe one horn, a good rhythm section, maybe some vibes. Yeah, that could be good.

I work so much with the girls that the jazz singing is a good break, because I'm not restricted by the arrangement, and I feel more free. When you have the girls and you got an arrangement, you always gotta hit the mark so other people sound like they're in the right place, too. It's kind of constraining.

The girls I have now sound good, though, don't get me wrong. It's hard to get women vocalists to make a good sound together, too. You can't just get singer A then add singer B and think you're gonna have something. It's kind of tricky. But if it's the right people, you can put a tune in front of somebody, play it once for them, and they can take it and swing, if they have swing in them. They're there in the moment as the changes go down, and can kind of predict where the tune is gonna go, and if you make a mistake they know to just keep playing until you make that mistake sound right, and that funny note begins to make sense.

DAN HICKS

I always tell the people in my band to communicate. That's what you want to do, that's the idea. If you're not communicating with the listener then you may be playing too busy, or playing too many notes. And whether you're playing or listening—but playing it, mainly—you want to get inside of it. That's part of the thing. You get inside it and you're in there and you're listening to everything and you're feeling it and it's affecting you. That's what you're always shooting for.

the best years
by kristine mckenna

Like anyone with an ounce of sense, I became a Dan Hicks fan the second I heard a note of his music in the early 70s. I was a teenager and I saw him on television and I was hooked. How could anyone resist Dan and his music?

Cut forward several decades and I'd become a writer, and it came to pass that Dan was writing a memoir and needed an editor. Needless to say, I was honored to serve. Dan began working on this memoir in the spring of 2013, and he put a lot of time into the book for the next six months. He'd completed six chapters by fall of that year when he was diagnosed with throat cancer, and work on the book was suspended while he focused on getting well. Dan and Clare tackled the cancer with great courage and determination, and by late spring of 2014 he'd gone into remission.

He was fragile, though, and he returned to the book with limited energy. Not knowing what the future might hold, I stepped in as his editor and made a suggestion. I felt it important that the book include a chapter where Dan spoke exclusively about music, and I encouraged him to write such a chapter, which he did. The plan at that point was to complete the book with a final chapter that brought the story up to the present.

Then, at the end of 2014, Dan was diagnosed with liver cancer, and the treatment this time was much tougher. He was still recovering from his previous bout with cancer and suddenly he was fighting a more aggressive one. Again, he and Clare jumped in with both feet in terms of treatment and they left no stone unturned in the effort to get Dan well. That wasn't to be; on February 6, 2016, the world lost a musical genius, and those of us who had the good fortune to know him lost someone who was deeply loved.

In an effort to tie up loose ends and complete Dan's memoir, *The Best Years* is an attempt to cover the last two decades of his life and finish the story. I titled this chapter *The Best Years* because I think these were the happiest years of his life.

♠

Marrying Clare Wasserman in 1996 was a huge turning point for Dan. He'd been in love with her for decades, she'd seen him through the worst period of his life, and she provided him with an anchor that he'd always needed. Although Dan stopped drinking in

1985 through Alcoholics Anonymous, he'd never really embraced the emotional recovery work that's central to the Alcoholics Anonymous Program. After marrying Clare, he began to do that work.

'There was a change in Dan starting in 1996,' Clare said. 'He'd danced around it before, but at that point the program became a core part of our lives and it transformed him. It gave his life back to him.'

When Dan married Clare he hadn't released a recording of new material for two decades and was making a living exclusively as a touring artist. He never really stopped being on the road; when he went on the road, however, it was always on his terms.

'Dan used to marvel at bands that would go out for weeks,' Clare recalled. 'If we could get him to go out for ten days we were lucky, and he was particular about how he toured, because he wanted to enjoy it. He would only drive a certain number of miles a day, would only fly at certain times, would only stay in certain hotels, and would never do press on the day of a show. He made it pleasurable because he couldn't present the work the way he wanted to if he was tired.

'Performing live was always the happiest thing for him because he was the master and he ran the show and he controlled it. You don't get to do that in a recording studio, but live it was his baby. Dan was essentially a jazz artist, so this wasn't party time, and he always had seated rooms because he wanted people to listen. Soundcheck had to be done at a certain time and a certain way, and everything led up to him being able to hit that stage and hear what he needed to hear.

'My job was to make sure everybody understood in advance what he needed, and if I was there and things were going well, he would get this little smile two or three songs into the set, and then I knew things were right. If I wasn't there I would hold my breath until he called me after the show. He could've cared less what *we* all thought, by the way. It was about whether they were making the sound *he* wanted to hear.'

In 1998, *Early Muses*, a compilation of Dan's solo recordings from the 60s, was released, and that same year his recording career resumed in earnest when Dave Kaplan, owner of Surfdog Records, came into his life. Born and raised in Phoenix, Kaplan is one of many people who were smitten with Dan when they saw him on television in the early 70s.

'I was just blown away,' Kaplan recalled, of seeing Dan on *The Tonight Show*. 'The next day I bugged my mom until she took me to the record store where I bought *Where's The Money?*, and to this day that's one of my all time favorite albums. I can't speak highly enough of it. It's just brilliant.'

Kaplan gravitated to Los Angeles during his twenties, and in 1984 he began managing the UK group UB40. That led to more managing gigs, and he was soon in charge of an extensive roster of artists. In 1993, he founded Surfdog Records, based in Encinitas, California, and five years later he made his way to Dan.

'One day a crewmember on the road with one of my bands said the name Dan Hicks. I turned around and said, "What are you saying about Dan Hicks?" This guy said, "I know Dan," and I said, "Can you get me in touch with him?" I got a meeting with Dan and flew up to Mill Valley, and we had a meal together and talked for hours, and that led to him signing with Surfdog.'

Thus began an enduring relationship that was to last through eighteen years and seven records. 'Dave spent way more than he ever made on Dan, and he gave him complete latitude,' Clare recalled. 'Dave was a real patron. He also has an amazing ear and knows his stuff and Dan respected that.'

Kaplan gave Dan *carte blanche*, but he did have specific things in mind when he signed him to Surfdog. 'I encouraged him to reform The Hot Licks,' said Kaplan. 'There's nothing like that sound! It was just so ingenious the way he built those vocals into a sound, and he said, "Yeah, let's do it." I think he'd been waiting for someone to ask. I didn't encourage this because it was a good commercial move, by the way. I wanted him to do it because it was so brilliant musically.'

The Hot Licks reformed for Dan's 2000 debut album on Surfdog, *Beatin' The Heat*, and the music had another intriguing element built into it, too. 'I knew that Dan had some pretty auspicious fans,' Kaplan said, 'and I asked him, "Have you ever asked any of them to sing with you?" He was very humble about it and said it hadn't really crossed his mind, and I said, "Do you mind if I ask?"

'He said no, so I did ask, and the response I got was unbelievable. First I'd get the lawyers and they'd say, "No, I don't think my client could do that"—then the minute word got to the artist that it was Dan asking, they'd respond instantly. Bette Midler was typical. She just said, "What does he want me to sing, where do you need me to be, and what time? I'll be there and do whatever he wants." That was basically the way it went with all of them.'

While they were gearing up for the record, Clare recalled Dan calling Tom Waits at home and leaving a message. 'Dan said, "I've got this record, I'd love you to come and do a tune." Waits called back and said, "Oh God, I've been doing all these guest spots, my label is really not happy, I don't think I can do another one." Fifteen minutes later, the phone rang and he left a message saying, "Fuck it, I'm doing it. What do you want me to do?" So they went up to this little studio in Sonoma and recorded "I'll Tell You Why That Is.'"

Kaplan remembered the making of the first album he did with Dan as a fairly dramatic experience. 'Dan came to some mixes early on and he was a super micro-manager,' he said. 'He's schooling everybody, and we can't get four seconds into the thing without nineteen changes, and we had the big showdown. I said, "Dan, you have to leave. We can't get this done."

'I had to legislate it in for all future records that Dan is not in the mix room. I told him, "I promise I'll change anything you don't like, but first you gotta let us do it!" He finally did leave, but he was downright angry when he heard the first mix of *Beatin' The Heat*. Then, somehow he came to the conclusion that what we were doing was OK, and he let us do it. The mix thing was always an issue, though, and thank god for Clare, the ultimate diplomat.

'Dan was a genius, humorous, the very definition of authentic, and a sweet, gentle soul and great human inside. But he was also downright scary and incredibly difficult in moments. He had that side, too, but it all added up to making him even more lovable because he was so real.'

Dan was energized by the making and release of *Beatin' The Heat*, and the following year he released a live album with Surfdog called *Alive & Lickin'*. 'Dan never cared about being catapulted back into stardom, but the fact that people were loving his music again excited him,' Kaplan said.

I SCARE MYSELF

The money part of his career revival meant nothing to him, however. 'The guy had a very strange sense of money,' Clare remembered. 'He could've owned a house but he couldn't care less about things like owning houses, and if it hadn't been for me he probably would've lived in a shack. He never had the aspirations many people have of owning things and he lived a very simple life based around the things he loved to do.

'He'd get a large chunk of money and I'd say, "We should save this," and he'd say, "Let's use it to live!" He didn't worry about the future because he was a bohemian and an artist, and money and career just didn't interest him. Dan would be invited to do things most artists would jump, at and his response would be, "Nah, I don't wanna do that." He walked away at the peak of his career and he did it willingly and really didn't care. David Allen, who ran the Boarding House where Dan and The Hot Licks played in the early days, once called Dan the most reluctant celebrity he'd ever met, and he was right.'

Dan was reluctant about the fame part, but he never held back when it came to the music. 'He was always writing, and he often went back to unfinished things he'd started decades earlier and finished them,' said Clare. 'For him, songwriting was hard and laborious, though, and he never understood it when people said, "Oh, I love to write songs!" He was arranging at the same time that he was writing, so writing meant he had to be thinking in orchestral terms, and that's not easy.'

Kaplan encouraged Dan to develop new material. 'He would send super-lo-fi cassettes of new songs, and it was always just him on the demo. I don't know how he did it, but I think he had two

173

cassette players, and he would sing the song on a cassette, and then sing along with that recording doing harmonies. It sounded like somebody singing into a recorder on the other side of the room, and you'd really have to use your imagination at that point, but the parts were all there, and the cassettes were just magical.'

♠

Those early years with Surfdog were productive ones for Dan; his creative life was pretty much exactly what he wanted it to be, and he had a daily routine that suited him. 'He always got up first, and he'd make coffee then he'd go sit down at his table and start to draw or cut things out,' said Clare. 'He always had a little project he was working on, whether it was a birthday card for someone or a flyer for one of his shows, and he was always engaged with something. He grew up in a military family and was very disciplined, and every day he made lists of what he had to get done in these spiral notebooks that were his journals.

'He loved to stand out on the deck, and there were birds and squirrels that would come, and he loved movies and he loved the Giants—he had this baseball mitt his father gave him, and he'd bring it out if the Giants were losing. We didn't really go out much, and the idea of having people over for a dinner party? There was no way that was gonna happen in our house. He'd say, "Why would we do that?"

'He wasn't a trivial guy. Dan was a real serious guy, he was very shy and easily bored, and his essential nature was solitary. One of the reasons he liked Mill Valley was because people there knew him and left him alone.'

I SCARE MYSELF

Dan liked to be left alone but he had a lot of friends, and on December 1, 2001, he invited all of them to join him onstage at San Francisco's Warfield Theater to celebrate his sixtieth birthday. Dan wanted everyone he'd ever played with to participate, and he rounded up dozens of people of varying musical ability. The concert was filmed and recorded and led to a CD/DVD package that was released in 2003. 'I had someone special, and that was a particularly special event,' Kaplan recalled. 'Of course I captured it!'

The following year saw the release of another record, *Selected Shorts*, which included two new songs and was produced by the late Tim Hauser, who co-founded the jazz group The Manhattan Transfer in 1969. Dan didn't have a good experience in the studio on this one, and didn't release another album for five years. But by 2009 he was ready to return to the studio to record *Tangled Tales*.

Various female vocalists served as Lickettes after Dan reformed the group in 1999, but the two who arrived in 2009—Roberta Donnay and Daria—were to remain with him for the remainder of his career, and they appear on record with Dan for the first time on this album.

'You could be the greatest virtuoso, but you weren't gonna be in Dan's band if he didn't get along with you,' said Clare. 'He auditioned people partly on their personalities. *Can I sit and talk to this person on a plane for a few hours?* Daria and Roberta were two of the best girls he ever had, live and in the studio. He related to them and they created the sound he wanted to hear.'

It was right around then that Dan threw off the shackles and dove fully into jazz. In 2010 he formed a quartet called Bayside Jazz, and he was strictly the vocalist in this lineup, which performed throughout the Bay Area for five years. 'Such is his dedication that Dan is making Bayside Jazz With Dan Hicks available at a *fraction* of his regular fee,' he announced on his website. 'He wants to get onstage!'

'Dan was in awe of great jazz singers and he worked really hard on singing,' Clare recalled. 'Doing the little jazz clubs was a joy for him because it was just him up there with the tunes. He lived for that. He'd get on the phone and call people and say, "Can I play your club?"'

Kaplan was aware that Dan's music was moving increasingly in the direction of pure jazz. 'Over the years his instincts were going increasingly down tempo and the music was getting more serious. I told him the records tend to get a little sleepy the way he was presenting them to me, and he was open to what I was saying, but if he'd had his druthers I think he would've delivered a jazz standards record.'

What a tragedy that we never got that record! We did, however, get what could be described as a jazz Christmas album in 2010, and it was a long and winding road that led him to it.

For a few months in 1977, Dan hosted Monday Night Open Mike at the Old Mill Tavern in Mill Valley. On December 19 of that year, an impromptu band got together there and performed a set of rewritten Christmas songs. Thus was born The Christmas Jug Band, a revolving crew of approximately a dozen musicians, and a tradition that's survived for four decades. The group released three albums between the years 1987 and 2014, and continues to perform.

Dan accumulated a repertoire of Christmas tunes as a result, and he teamed up with The Hot Licks and several players from Bayside Jazz to make *Crazy For Christmas*.

176

¡ Viva Tequila !

Jaco y Jaime y Dan en Cantine Tenampa MEXiCO CiTy MAY 11, 1973

Dan in Tijuana with friends
Jaime Leopold and Jaco
Morgenstern, May 11, 1973.

LEFT Fingers up: Bobby Black, Dan, and Dave Bell onstage at the 142 Throckmorton Theatre, Mill Valley, California, April 8, 2006. BELOW A stage set decorated with items from Dan's collection.

Dan onstage at the Palm Ballroom in San Raphael, California, during one of his 'Kollege of Musical Knowledge' shows, March 2011. *Left to right*: Tim Eschliman, Roberta Donnay, Daria, Jimmy Dillon, Dan, Brian Simpson, Paul Robinson.

ABOVE Clare and Dan at the Sonoma Mission Inn on Sara Wasserman's birthday, 2011. **OPPOSITE** Clare Wasserman Hicks in Healdsburg on her and Dan's wedding anniversary, May 14, 2011.

142 Throckmorton Theatre

SNEAK PEEK

SATURDAY

March 8th

DAN HICKS and the hot licks

A concert of new material–Plus some past gems!

8PM Sharp!

142 Throckmorton Theatre, Mill Valley
www.142ThrockmortonTheatre.org • 415.383.9600

©2008 142 Throckmorton Theatre • Design by Dan Hicks & Megan Aola • Printed by WIGT.com

OPPOSITE One of the hundreds of handmade promotional mailers Dan designed. ABOVE Dan during a recording session in Los Angeles, 2004. LEFT Another of Dan's mailers.

The concert at Davies Symphony Hall to celebrate Dan's seventieth birthday in 2013. *Left to right*: Daria, Maria Muldaur, Sara Wasserman, Roberta Donnay, Naomi Eisenberg, Paul Robinson, Jaime Leopold, Brian Simpson, Dan Hicks, Paul Smith, Sid Page, David Grisman, Benito Cortez, Jon Weber, Roy Rogers, Bruce Forman, Rickie Lee Jones, Ray Benson, Patti Cathcart Andress, Turtle VanDeMarr, Ramblin' Jack Elliott, William Charles 'Tuck' Andress, and Lowell 'Banana' Levinger.

189

OPPOSITE Dan in San Rafael, 2009.
BELOW Dan with items from the
collection of Mickey McGowan, 2009.
FOLLOWING PAGE Dan in 2004.

'Dan loved Christmas and loved making that album,' Clare recalled. 'He wanted to rewrite an old Christmas standard that Paul McCartney's publishing company, MPL Communications, controlled, and he had to get permission to rewrite it. I called and talked to the head honcho, and she went and talked to McCartney, then she came back and said, "For Dan? You got it. Just send us a copy."

'That record took off, too, and it charted on *Billboard*—everybody was shocked. He got some of the best reviews he'd ever had, and it was in the *New York Times* list of the top ten Christmas records.'

In 2011, Dan had a seventieth birthday gathering at Davies Symphony Hall in San Francisco, and everybody showed up for this one, too, including Van Dyke Parks, Rickie Lee Jones, Harry Shearer, Maria Muldaur, and Jim Kweskin. The lineup was impressive, and that show too was recorded and released as an album early in 2013.

Then everything changed.

'In the fall he got a sore throat, and we went to a Marin County doctor who told him he had some digestive problem,' Clare remembered. 'The sore throat didn't go away, though, so he went into the hospital and had a biopsy, and afterwards the same doctor came into the room and said, "It's cancer, you have to call Stanford immediately."

'It was seven in the morning, and that was the beginning of a very long road. We immediately went to Stanford, and he saw a throat surgeon named Dr. Kaplan who was amazing. Dr. Kaplan said, "You have stage four throat cancer. This is what we can do, and I think we can bring you through it and you can recover." Dan just looked at him and said OK. We left the building and were walking

DAN HICKS

to the car, and he looked at me and said, "Well, that didn't go like we planned!"

'At that point our lives became focused on doing exactly what the doctors instructed and doing everything right. He listened to every doctor, did what he was asked, went to his treatment, and he was astounding. All the way through he maintained our lives, and you'd never have known to look at him that he was fighting cancer. He loved his life, and he continued doing exactly what he'd always done, and he enjoyed himself, and he never complained or said, "Poor me." He took some really hard blows, too. The radiation left him with fourth degree burns and he put up with a lot.

'We always had goals we were working toward, and the thing that carried him through the throat cancer was a Fats Waller tribute show he'd booked at the SFJAZZ Center. Every day he got up and worked on the show, and that kept him focused. He did arranging and made tapes for the band, and he found a way to sing from a different place in his throat. He was determined to do that show and he performed it with a tube in his stomach. He was still on a feeding tube the night of the show.'

The Fats Waller show, which took place on May 21, 2014, was exquisite and quietly perfect. Waller's material took Dan exactly where he wanted to go musically, and his renditions of 'Honeysuckle Rose,' 'Ain't Misbehavin',' and 'Jitterbug Waltz,' among others, were breathtakingly beautiful and seemingly effortless. The sense of ease and pleasure that always informed Dan's music was a direct result of the endless hours he put into it.

'The throat cancer was a viral cancer, which has a much better recovery rate than you have with many cancers, and it was fully expected that he would recover from this,' Clare continued. 'And there was a respite from April to early January of the next year. Then, while they were doing a full-body scan to check his throat, they found a lump on the liver. I texted Dr. Kaplan immediately, and twenty-four hours later we were at Stanford with a team of five doctors.

'We never went into paroxysms of panic and grief—never went there. It was always, *OK, this is what's happening, and this is what we're going to do*. One question at that point was how to create a treatment plan that wouldn't force us to cancel the Charlatans fiftieth-year reunion that had been scheduled for that June. The idea was to take this tumor out, so we did two preliminary procedures to pre-treat the cancer prior to surgery and he sailed through both of them. Those were in April and May, during the period when he was rehearsing with The Charlatans.

'The Charlatans were a hard bunch to corral, but Dan loved these guys. He was always happy when their work came forward and loved being with them, and they adored him. It was a job to put these guys back together musically, though, and when it was decided that The Charlatans were doing a show he knew he'd kind of have to run things. I heard him on the phone with Mike Wilhelm saying, "OK I'm gonna commit to one rehearsal and that's all," but he hung in, and thirteen rehearsals later he was still working with them. They always rehearsed at George's house in Sonoma, and he'd come home and say, "My god, they're talking all the time!" This is a guy who ran a really tight ship with his band, but he loosened up for The Charlatans because they were family.'

DAN HICKS

The reunion show took place in Virginia City on June 20, 2015, and it was everything one might expect. Dan was very thin at that point—still dressed to the nines, of course—and the music was charming, nostalgic, extremely loose. As The Charlatans' ramshackle set wound to a close, Dan stepped to the front of the stage, sat down on a stool, and with a wry smile that seemed to say, *OK folks, this is how it's done*, casually knocked a tune out of the ballpark. I can't recall exactly what the song was—a simple bit of Americana, some traditional folk tune—but it was swinging and flawless. Dan was such a pro and had such respect for music; he never gave it short shrift.

Two weeks after that show, Dan had his liver surgery.

'That's when our lives really changed,' Clare recalled. 'You're not a candidate for a liver transplant if you've had cancer within four years because of the drugs involved, and apparently Dan needed a new liver. I don't know how much of this he knew, but *I* knew because I stayed up all night doing research on the internet. Dan always had high hopes and faith in people, so he went in and had this long surgery, and afterwards they called and said, "I think we got everything." And we thought we were done.

'But we weren't done. The liver cancer returned with a vengeance, and when that hit Dan he looked at me, I'll never forget it, and for the first time he said, "I'm scared." I said, "It's OK, I'm here, I go where you go and we're always together."

'I think that gave him permission to let go. I'd been the fighter for so long, always challenging the doctors and investigating alternatives and unwilling to stop, and he needed to know it was OK to finally let go. He was in bed that last time we talked, and afterwards he just

196

closed his eyes and folded his hands on his chest, then he went to sleep for a couple of days and just slipped away. There was never a sign of pain or struggle and it was a good leaving. We had his favorite jazz going, close family and friends with us, and his doggie was at the foot of his bed. He was an absolute prince through the whole thing, and I have such admiration for what he did and how he did it. He always had the greatest grace and integrity about everything.'

Grace is a good word with regard to Dan; he was a cool character, and music flowed from him with such elegance and style. He dug what he did, he dug what his life came to stand for, and he dug the way he lived it.

'We'd drive over the bridge, whether it was to the Warfield Theater for his sixtieth birthday show or Davies Hall for the sixtieth, and we'd be in the Caddy and it would be full of things he was gonna put onstage, these big figures, and the back seat of the car was like a crazy, traveling antique store, and we'd pull up and he'd say, "OK, we're going in. See you on the other side,"' Clare remembered. 'Afterwards he'd say, "We did it!" And we'd always have to stop on the way home at the 7–11 in Mill Valley and get some horrible donut or awful ice cream bar, but that was his victory pop. Then he'd hit the bed and close his eyes. I'd look over at him and marvel and say, "How did this one human being create all these worlds? All of this happened from a little vision going on in your head!"

'We all worked hard and a lot of people contributed, but it all started inside Dan. He'd just look over at me and smile.'

an afterword by tommy lipuma

When Dan's wife, Clare, called me and asked if I would write the epilogue for Dan's book, I was both honored and frightened by what seemed like a daunting task. To write about a man who was bigger than life is a huge undertaking. I stared at the page for a while, and then in my mind's ear I heard Dan telling me with that sarcastic wise guy voice he sometimes used to get a point across to me, 'Don't be a chickenshit, man, just write what you feel.'

So I guess I'll start from the beginning.

I first met Dan in 1970. I don't know who originally hipped me to him, but I believe a demo tape of the new and improved Hot Licks that someone sent me was what first caught my ear. The songwriting and the vocal style got my curiosity up, so I did some homework and discovered he'd been the drummer in a San Francisco group called The Charlatans. Then I got his first album with The Hot Licks on Epic Records and discovered a few more knockout songs that he'd written, among them 'I Scare Myself' and 'Canned Music.' That was enough to convince me I had to meet this man.

I called him, and my partner, Bob Krasnow, and I agreed to fly up to San Francisco and meet him at his home, which was a houseboat at Pier 5, I believe. When we arrived at the pier it was a challenge just to find the boat, as he hadn't given me directions and cell phones hadn't been invented yet. When we finally found his residence, we discovered we had to walk across a plank that was approximately eight to ten feet long and eight to ten inches wide that stretched from the dock to the boat. The plank had bowed from usage, so midway across was three or four inches underwater that you had to step over. Just about where your foot would land beyond the submerged plank was a good sized dog turd, so you had to step just a little bit further to make it over the pile of shit Dan's dog, Fetch, had left as a calling card to avoid falling into the drink.

My first reaction was to laugh, as I thought this couldn't have been just an accidental mishap. Later, I wondered if it was some kind of test designed to gage how serious you were in pursuing him.

We became good friends, to the extent that he would stay at our home when he was in LA. I told Clare that we couldn't believe how tidy he would leave the guest room. The bed was made so perfectly that you could bounce a quarter off of it. Later, when Dan told me his father was a career army man, it all made sense.

DAN HICKS

When my wife, Gill, became pregnant with our second child, we decided to name it after Dan. Our daughter's name is Danielle, and every time Dan and I spoke, he would ask me, 'How's what's-her-name doing?'

It's not easy to peg Dan's music to a specific genre. First of all, his musical influences were so deep and wide. It would be easy to say he fits into the swing era, but then you listen to 'Moody Richard' or 'Reelin' Down' or 'I Scare Myself' and you realize he couldn't be pegged. He was a genuine original. There were times when I thought it was unfortunate that he didn't allow himself to reach the heights I know he could have reached, but he didn't want to drink the Kool-Aid, and I respected him for it.

He was a pretty private person who moved on his schedule, not someone else's.

I once told him he reminded me of the 1950s humorist Herb Shriner—if Shriner had taken acid.

When Dan passed, I received a letter of condolence from Elvis Costello, a mutual friend of ours who'd performed on one of Dan's later albums. He brought up an astute point. If I may quote him:

> There is such a lot of soul in his songs, and I wonder sometimes if the very stagecraft that made him so appealing to me when I first picked up *Where's The Money?* might have made less curious people think this was just a novelty act and miss the depth of his songs.

Elvis also mentioned that he'd posted his own salute to Dan on his Facebook page. The responses he received included one anecdote that really typified Dan for me. Again, I quote:

> Dear Elvis: Thanks so much for your words about Dan. In 1989 I asked him after a show, what should I listen to? He was not that friendly and walked away. He then walked by me and abruptly pushed a piece of paper in my hand without saying anything. It said LISTEN in capital letters, and it was underlined. Then it said Django, Fats Waller, Bob Wills & The Texas Playboys, Sons Of The Pioneers, It was a huge gateway for me.

This really struck me, as it was such a great insight into the man. Trying to get past that veneer was no easy task, but once you did, you found this very sensitive, beautiful human being who only wanted to feel the good things in life, which to him were music, a good book, friends, and his family. He had a very low threshold for bullshit, which meant he didn't tolerate it. To give you an example: he once stayed at our home in LA at a time when I happened to have a young nephew staying with me who was trying to break into the music business. We had a sauna in our backyard and Dan, my nephew, and I were taking a sauna together. During that visit, Dan experienced the Sicilian *padrone* streak I inherited from my father, which peeked its ugly head out while I was speaking to my nephew: 'Do this,' 'Get me that,' etc. While we were in the sauna I got thirsty, and I said to my nephew, 'Get me some water.' Dan piped up, 'Hey man, why don't you get your own fucking water?'

It was the reality check I needed to realize that the asshole in me needed a readjustment. Dan had that effect on people.

A few years ago, Gill and I had the good fortune of seeing Dan

DAN HICKS

perform in Fairfield, Connecticut, at the Warehouse, a great showcase club that holds seventy-five to a hundred people. It was packed with rabid fans who shouted and applauded before and after each song. They loved him.

I would like to note that the audience wasn't all aging baby boomers. There were enough young people in the audience to give me a sense that some younger music lovers got his message, too, and that this great man's music will live on.

In closing, I'd like to say that Dan was short on bullshit and long on talent, and I loved him like a brother.

TOMMY LIPUMA
POUND RIDGE, NEW YORK
NOVEMBER 2016

discography by kristine mckenna

All songs by Dan Hicks except as noted.

Beginning in 1978, with *It Happened One Bite*, Hicks often wrote liner notes for his recordings; his notes are included here as they originally appeared.

ORIGINAL RECORDINGS (1969)
DAN HICKS & HIS HOT LICKS
Produced by Bob Johnston.

While still a member of The Charlatans, Dan began doing shows with his own band, Dan Hicks & His Hot Licks. This album chronicling the early Hot Licks period is essentially a blueprint for what was to come. Overseen by Bob Johnston, a celebrity producer who'd just done four albums with Bob Dylan prior to going into the studio with Dan, *Original Recordings* is a poorly produced album, and the songs simply don't sound as rich and full as they do in later versions. There's excessive echo on several tracks, and Dan's vocals sound young; his pitch is a bit wobbly here and there, too, and that's something you'll never find in any of his subsequent recordings. Dan was already a surprisingly mature songwriter, though—he came out of the gate writing great tunes—and two of this signature songs, 'I Scare Myself' and 'Canned Music,' appear here for the first time. Also here is the first song he ever wrote, 'How Can I Miss You When You Won't Go Away?' A handful of vinyl pressings have surfaced that list the final track on the album, 'Jukie's Ball,' as 'Junkie's Ball.' Hicks looks darn cute in the cover photo, decked out in western gear. That's his beloved dog Fetch—offspring of the Family Dog's dog—at his feet.

■ THE PERSONNEL

Dan Hicks vocals, rhythm guitar, harmonica, drums
Jon Weber lead guitar
Sid Page violin

Sherry Snow vocals
Christina Vila Gancher vocals, celeste, piano
Jaime Leopold bull fiddle

■ THE TUNES

1 'Canned Music'
2 'How Can I Miss You When You Won't Go Away?'
3 'I Scare Myself'
4 'Shorty Takes A Dive'
5 'Evenin' Breeze'
6 'Waitin' For The 103'
7 'Shorty Falls In Love'
8 'Milk Shakin' Mama'
9 'Slow Movin''
10 'It's Bad Grammar, Baby'

WHERE'S THE MONEY? (1972)
DAN HICKS & HIS HOT LICKS
Produced by Tommy LiPuma.
Recorded at the Troubadour, Los Angeles, February 1971.

Recorded live at the Troubadour in Los Angeles, *Where's The Money?* is where anyone new to Dan's music should start. It's all here, gloriously perfect, for the first time: witty tunes, brilliant arrangements, gorgeous vocals, impeccable musicianship, and Dan's irresistible stage persona. Dan had fabulous comic timing and could think on his feet, and his stage patter and exchanges with audience members are invariably memorable. Featuring what's come to be regarded as the classic Hot Licks lineup, *Where's The Money?* was Dan's breakout album, and it features two of the greatest songs in his canon: 'Shorty Falls In Love' and 'The Buzzard Was Their Friend.' The lyrics to both of these very fast songs are really clever, and these live versions are flawless.

I SCARE MYSELF

Several women performed as Lickettes over the years, but Maryann Price was arguably the best of them, and her very hip vocal on 'Shorty Falls In Love' is sensational. Dan loved scat singing, and it's front and center here, and on all the music that was to follow.

The album was produced by the masterful Tommy LiPuma, a seasoned music man whose roots are in jazz. LiPuma understood that Dan wanted his music to swing, which is a very particular approach to rhythm, and he knew how to capture it in a recording. Together, he and Dan created a work of genius.

■ THE PERSONNEL

Dan Hicks vocals, guitar

Naomi Ruth Eisenberg vocals, percussion, second fiddle

Maryann Price vocals, percussion

Sid Page violin, mandolin, vocals

Jaime Leopold double bass

■ THE TUNES

1 'I Feel Like Singing'
2 'Coast To Coast'
3 'News From Up The Street'
4 'Where's The Money?'
5 'Caught In The Rain'
6 'Shorty Falls In Love'

7 'By Hook Or By Crook'
8 'Reelin' Down'
9 'The Buzzard Was Their Friend'
10 'Traffic Jam'
11 'Is This My Happy Home?'
12 'Dig A Little Deeper'

STRIKING IT RICH (1972)
DAN HICKS & HIS HOT LICKS
Produced by Tommy LiPuma.
Recorded at Sunset Sound, Los Angeles, January and February 1972.

The second album to showcase Dan operating on all cylinders, *Striking It Rich* includes the definitive recordings of 'Canned Music,' a dreamy song that seems to tip-toe into earshot, and the sensual love song 'I Scare Myself.' Also here is an early, previously unrecorded song, 'Moody Richard (The Innocent Bystander),' and three of Dan's finest songs, 'Woe, The Luck,' 'Walkin' One And Only,' and 'You Got To Believe'; all of them have a unique charm that's distinctly Hicksian. Featuring the

DAN HICKS

classic Hot Licks lineup, the album also finds LiPuma on board again; Dan really liked him, and the record has a joyful quality that reflects that.

■ THE PERSONNEL

Dan Hicks vocals, rhythm guitar

Naomi Ruth Eisenberg vocals, second violin, percussion

Maryann Price vocals, percussion

Sid Page violin

John Girton lead guitar

Jaime Leopold string bass

■ THE TUNES

1 'You Got To Believe'
2 'Walkin' One And Only'
3 'O'Reilly At The Bar'
4 'Moody Richard (The Innocent Bystander)'
5 'Flight Of The Fly' (by John Girton)
6 'I Scare Myself'
7 'Philly Rag' (by John Girton)
8 'The Laughing Song'
9 'Canned Music'
10 'I'm An Old Cowhand (From The Rio Grande)' (by Johnny Mercer)
11 'Woe, The Luck'
12 'Presently In The Past' (by Naomi Ruth Eisenberg)
13 'Skippy's Farewell'
14 'Fujiyama' (by John Girton)

LAST TRAIN TO HICKSVILLE: THE HOME OF HAPPY FEET (1973)
DAN HICKS & HIS HOT LICKS
Produced by Tommy LiPuma.

The last of Dan's albums on Blue Thumb Records, *Last Train To Hicksville* includes ''Long Come A Viper,' a song he wrote while he was in The Charlatans. Performing this song was nothing short of an athletic feat; the lyrics are complicated, the tempo is insanely fast, and Dan nails it with apparent ease. Also here is 'The Euphonious Whale,' which has the quality of a sophisticated nursery rhyme, the charming love song 'My Old Timey Baby,' and 'Payday Blues,' which was always a crowd-pleaser in his live shows.

The real jewel of the album is 'It's Not My Time To Go,' a sad song Dan rarely performed live, but is one of his greatest compositions. There are a few oddities here: 'Success,' a song written and performed by Naomi Ruth Eisenberg, sounds nothing like Dan's material, and an instrumental by John Girton doesn't quite fit, either. This record was the last hurrah for the classic Hot Licks lineup, and you can feel that in the vibe of the record.

■ THE PERSONNEL

Dan Hicks vocals, rhythm guitar

Maryann Price vocals

John Girton lead guitar, dobro

Naomi Eisenberg vocals, violin

Jaime Leopold string bass

Bob Scott drums

Sid Page lead violin, mandolin

■ THE TUNES

1 'Cowboy's Dream #19'
2 'Lonely Madman'
3 'My Old Timey Baby'
4 'Vivando' (by John Girton)
5 'Success' (by Naomi Ruth Eisenberg)
6 'Cheaters Don't Win'
7 'Payday Blues'
8 'I Asked My Doctor'
9 'Sure Beats Me'
10 'The Euphonious Whale'
11 'Sweetheart (Waitress In A Donut Shop)' (by Ken Burgan)
12 ''Long Come A Viper'
13 'It's Not My Time To Go'

IT HAPPENED ONE BITE (1978)
DAN HICKS

Original album produced by Tommy LiPuma and Dan Hicks.
'Widescreen Edition' tracks produced by Dan Hicks. Recorded at the Record Plant, 1976.
Japanese CD release 2000; US re-release with bonus tracks 2001.

This isn't billed as a Hot Licks record, but it actually sounds like one; although there is no violin (a key element in the Hot Licks sound), Dan's interplay with a pair of female vocalists is a prominent part of many tunes, and that was one of the cornerstones of the Hot Licks style.

Comprising music Dan composed for Ralph Bakshi's film *Hey Good Lookin'*, *It*

DAN HICKS

Happened One Bite was released by Warner Brothers despite the fact that the film was shelved. Highlights include a charming cover of the Carroll Gibbons standard 'Garden In The Rain,' and 'Lovers For Life,' a song with a fabulous bridge and a lilting, irresistible melody. Also here is one of Dan's loveliest songs, 'Cloud My Sunny Mood,' which has a quality of wistful resignation that takes on added poignancy when you realize what was going on in his life when he wrote it. He was beginning a downward spiral into substance abuse and struggling with the depression that invariably accompanies that experience; you can hear that in the tune.

In 2001, Rhino Records, a subsidiary of Warner Brothers, released the 'Widescreen Edition' of It Happened One Bite. Produced by Roland Worthington Hand, this version tacks on several previously unreleased tracks that were recorded at the Record Plant in Sausalito, California, in 1976. Among them are freewheeling covers of the standards 'It's Only A Paper Moon' and 'Lulu's Back In Town.' Dan was clearly in his cups during the Record Plant sessions, and he expressed regret over the release of the bonus tracks, which he felt weren't up to his standards. (They aren't.) 'I think I even said the F-word,' he once ruefully pointed out. Actually, the version of 'Hummin' To Myself' recorded during those sessions is excellent, and captures guitarist John Girton in particularly fine form. The cover art is by Dan, who also wrote an alternate plot for the film that's reprinted below.

■ THE STORY

Did you know? This entire album was recorded in just ninety-two minutes flat! You see, back in 1975, Dan Hicks was commissioned by Ralph Bakshi, of Fritz The Cat and Heavy Traffic fame, to compose the music for his new full-length animated Feature film, Hey Good Lookin'. So they sat Dan down with his guitar and showed him the musicless film one-time through as he extemporaneously played and sang the songs on this album into a tape recorder. The film lasted eighty-five minutes. The remaining seven minutes were used to 'dub' in the other instrumentalists and singers (curiously sounding like the group Dan Hicks & His Hot Licks, but not so curious at that … as that is the 'sound' which was desired for the film). Amazing feat, isn't it? Not only that but someone somewhere decided not to release the film! Hey, but no fault of the music, as one casual listen to this stuff will testify. No film … but plenty of soundtrack! How 'bout it? Soundtrack in search of a movie? Hey, that's no way to run a pizza parlour. And no way these tunes were going to sit in the 'can' forever, so here they are! And with all these titles there's got to be a story in there somewhere. Heck,

208

I SCARE MYSELF

there's a trillion stories on this funny old globe … so let's jump into this story and see what happens … to you.

So there you are. It's 1956 and you're behind the wheel of your 1972 Chevy Corvette just cruzin' over the Grandma's house up in Blasted Canyon. It's not a long ride (just over two minutes and forty-five seconds).' 'Yeah! Vinnie's Lookin' Good,' you say to yourself as Vinnie—the young, well-built hired hand for Grandma's ranch—opens the front gate for you. As his greasy black hair gleams in all its brilliance in your rear-view mirror you wonder just what he looks like in pajamas. But shame on you for such thoughts, 'cause it's time to see Grandma!

Grandma, the sweet thing, comes to the door in her favorite Tex Beneke overalls and announces they're all out of vermouth, so no Harvey Wallbangers today; which reminds her the garden needs watering, but you reply, 'It's raining today Grandma,' so you both step outside to catch the 'Garden In The Rain.'

Bing! Bang! Wow, Grandma's hundred-year-old grandfather clock on the wall is still ticking away as good as ever! But, my gawd, it's late and you must be going. But old Granny insists you stay for dinner, which is—thanks to Vinnie picking up the wrong food coloring—Collared Blues! And the blues is what you got after eating, but you don't say anything because now Grandma is reminiscing about Grandpa, which always cues the photo albums and a running narrative over their halcyon days when they were both young and promised to be Lovers For Life.

The plot thickens with a loud war whoop when Vinnie calls from the bunk house to say that tomorrow is Sunday and, oh boy, he gets to read the Sunday funnies! Understanding Grandma alludes to the fact that Vinnie's not really playing with a full deck when she tells you the kids at his remedial night school call him Crazy, 'Cause He Is. Well, now it is time for you to get out of there and you forget all about pajamas, gardens, and Grandfather clocks and make one straight bee-line for your Corvette! Long good-byes you never liked and you breath introspectively, Mama, I'm An Outlaw as you take that 15mph hairpin turn down the mountain at a ballsy 45, howling at the moon in wild anticipation of the sights and the sounds of Saturday night in the Big City!

First Stop!: Shorty's Bar and Grill … ah, the old standby. As Louise, the hat check girl, checks your hat … coat, skirt, blouse, nylons, bra, panties, and platforms it dawns on you, 'Boy, has Shorty's changed!' This is exactly the action you were looking for, but some three-foot Albino cretin keeps tugging at your purse and insisting You Belong To Me. Well, you cool his jets with a quick trip to the powder

DAN HICKS

room to, uh, freshen up. Of course the powder room is packed and there's nothing for you but Waitin' … to the sounds of flushing toilets and sniffing noses. Oh, if only Grandma could see you now, and not all those other people.

At last, it's your turn and just as you're finished, uh, freshening up, somebody yells 'Raid!!' and you know they are not hawking a cockroach exterminator as you ditch swiftly out the back door and slip safely into your car. Well, sort of safely, since all you're wearing is your car keys.

Laying rubber and extremely undaunted by the busy Saturday night traffic and the mayhem you are creating you say, 'No way, Jose, is this going to Cloud My Sunny Mood,' and set your sites straight for home sweet home. No sooner said than done and what a wonderful sight home is too! And there's your pet canary Boogaloo chirping off a string of Johnny Mathis hits, and you feel warm all over.

Hey! Right into bed and four blissful hours in the arms of Morpheus, the one and only Deity of Dreams, only to be awakened by your trusty Bell and Howell clock-radio with its favorite early morning program Reveille Revisited. And it's 'up-and-at-'em' and off to work to the Pizza Parlour where your boss is already mad because you're probably late.

Now there's a story!

And what's this got to do with the album's cover design and its title, *It Happened One Bite?* Oh, that's another story.

■ THE PERSONNEL (ORIGINAL ALBUM)

Dan Hicks vocals, rhythm guitar, coffee pot
Maryann Price vocals
John Girton lead and rhythm guitar, vocal harmonies
Sid Page violin

Richard Borden drums
Lyle Ritz string bass, ukulele
Clarence McDonald keyboards
Michael Franks banjo
Gerry Stenholtz percussion
Bill Dickenson electric bass

■ THE TUNES (ORIGINAL ALBUM)

1 'Cruzin''
2 'Crazy 'Cause He Is'
3 'Garden In The Rain'
4 'Boogaloo Jones'
5 'Cloud My Sunny Mood'
6 'Dizzy Dogs'
7 'Vinnie's Lookin' Good'
8 'Lovers For Life'
9 'Collared Blues'
10 'Waitin''

210

11 'Reville Revisited'
12 'Mama, I'm An Outlaw'

13 'Boogaloo Plays Guitar'

■ THE PERSONNEL (WIDESCREEN EDITION)

Dan Hicks vocals, rhythm guitar

Maryann Price vocals

John Girton lead and rhythm guitar, vocals

Jeff Neighbor bass guitar

Mitch Woods piano

Bob Scott drums

■ THE TUNES (WIDESCREEN EDITION)

As above, plus

14 'You Belong To Me' (by King/Price/ Stewart)

15 'Mama, I'm An Outlaw' (slow version)

16 'Vinnie's Lookin' Good' (slow version)

17 'Gone With The Wind' (by Magidson/Wrubel)

18 'Walkin' My Baby Back Home' (by Ahlert/Turk)

19 'It's Only A Paper Moon' (by Arlen/ Harburg/Rose)

20 'Honeysuckle Rose' (by Razaf/Waller)

21 'Lulu's Back In Town' (by Dubin/ Harry)

22 'Hummin' To Myself'

SHOOTIN' STRAIGHT (1994)
DAN HICKS & THE ACOUSTIC WARRIORS

Produced by Joel Moss.

Recorded live at McCabe's Guitar Shop, Los Angeles.

A live album recorded at McCabe's Guitar Shop in Santa Monica, California, *Shootin' Straight* was released by On The Spot, a division of Private Music, and is currently out of print. This was Dan's first recording to include guitarist Paul Robinson, a gifted musician who became a mainstay for Dan, who clearly admired his playing. This was a shaky period for Dan; he was still struggling with his sobriety, and had mixed feelings about live performances. He's completely on point, funny and confident here, though, and his voice sounds great. The album introduces several new songs, including the novelty tunes, 'Up! Up! Up!' and 'Hell I'd Go.' Dan's novelty tunes were popular—his

211

DAN HICKS

live audiences always responded to them—but his genius resided in much more than his ability to make people laugh. That was part of it, yes, but his gifts as a writer, singer, and player are the main ingredients, and they come together exquisitely here in 'The Magician,' a mournful song about lost love, and 'Bottoms Up,' a drinking song awash in regret. Also here are three of the rapid-fire tongue twisters—'Willie,' '13-D,' and 'Who Are You'—that pretty much nobody but Dan could sing.

■ THE PERSONNEL

Dan Hicks vocals, rhythm guitar   **Alex Baum** string bass
Paul Robinson lead guitar   **Stevie Blacke** lead mandolin, fiddle
Jim Boggio jazz accordion, piano   **Bob Scott** drums (added during mixing)

■ THE TUNES

1 'Up! Up! Up!'
2 'Shootin' Straight'
3 'Hell, I'd Go!'
4 'Bottoms Up!'
5 'Texas Kinda' Attitude'
6 'Willie'
7 'Savin' My Lovin''
8 '13-D'
9 'Barstool Boogie'
10 'A Magician'
11 'Who Are You?'
12 'Level With Me Laurie'
13 'The Rounder'
14 '$100,000'

THE AMAZING CHARLATANS (1996)
THE CHARLATANS

Widely regarded as San Francisco's first psychedelic band, The Charlatans helped usher in the era of large-scale rock concerts fueled by LSD. The band went into the studio for several recording sessions between the years 1965 and 1968, and released a single on Kapp Records ('The Shadow Knows' b/w '32–20'), but could never get much traction on the commercial front. Dan's musicianship was developing at a rapid pace during this period, though. He started out as the drummer in the band, but was soon providing original material and lead vocals, and by 1968 he'd outgrown The Charlatans and left to form The Hot Licks.

This selection of Charlatans material, compiled by Alec Palao, includes three of

212

I SCARE MYSELF

Dan's songs that he subsequently recorded with The Hot Licks. With the exception of Richard Olsen, who co-wrote two songs here, Dan was the only band member contributing original material.

■ THE PERSONNEL

Dan Hicks drums, guitar, lead vocal on tracks marked *

George Hunter percussion, Autoharp, vocals

Michael Ferguson piano, keyboards, drums (tracks 1–20)

Richard Olsen bass, woodwinds, vocals

Mike Wilhelm lead guitar, vocals

Lynne Hughes guitar, vocals (tracks 5–13)

Patrick Gogerty keyboards (tracks 21–22)

Terry Wilson drums (tracks 21–22)

Hank Bradley violin (tracks 21–22)

■ THE TUNES

1 'Blues Ain't Nothin'
2 'Number One'
3 'Jack Of Diamonds' (traditional)
4 'Baby Won't You Tell Me'
5 'Alabama Bound'* (traditional)
6 ''Long Come A Viper'* (by Dan Hicks)
7 'By Hook Or By Crook'* (by Dan Hicks)
8 'I Saw Her' (traditional)
9 'Codine Blues' (by Buffy Sainte-Marie)
10 'Devil Got My Man' (by Nehemiah James & Skip James)
11 'Sidetrack' (traditional)
12 '32–20 Blues' (by Robert Johnson)
13 'The Shadow Knows' (by Jerry Leiber & Mike Stoller)
14 'Groom N' Clean'
15 'How Can I Miss You When You Won't Go Away?'* (by Dan Hicks)
16 'We're Not On The Same Trip'* (by Dan Hicks)
17 'Sweet Sue, Just You' (by Will J. Harris and Victor Young)
18 'I Always Wanted A Girl Like You' (by Ian Hunter and Richard Olsen)
19 'Alabama Bound' (traditional)
20 'Walkin'' (by Ian Hunter and Richard Olsen)
21 'I Got Mine'* (by Dan Hicks)
22 'Steppin' In Society' (by Harry Akst)
23 'East Virginia' (traditional)

■ ADDITIONAL NOTES

Tracks 1–4: Autumn Records demo session recorded at Coast Recorders, San Francisco, August 10, 1965, produced by Sly Stewart. Tracks 5–13: Kama Sutra

213

DAN HICKS

album sessions recorded at Coast Recorders, November 1–2 and December 3, 1965, produced by Erik Jacobsen. Track 14: jingle session for McCann-Erickson ad agency, Golden State Recorders, San Francisco, November 16, 1966. Tracks 15–20 produced by The Charlatans for Bravado Productions, recorded at Golden State Recorders, San Francisco, July 17–18, 1967. Tracks 21–23 produced by The Charlatans at Pacific High Recorders, Sausalito, 1968. 'The Shadow Knows' / '32–20' was released as a single on Kapp Records (#779) in October 1966. Mono mixes of selected tracks, along with an alternate version of 'I Saw Her' featured on *The Limit Of The Marvelous* (Big Beat HIQLP 035), were released in 2016.

RETURN TO HICKSVILLE (THE BEST OF DAN HICKS & HIS HOT LICKS: THE BLUE THUMB YEARS, 1971–1973) (1997)
DAN HICKS & HIS HOT LICKS

■ THE PERSONNEL
Dan Hicks vocals, guitar, percussion overdubs
Maryann Price vocals, percussion
Naomi Ruth Eisenberg vocals, percussion, second fiddle
Sid Page violin, occasional harmony

Jaime Leopold string bass
John Girton lead guitar, lap steel (tracks 7–13), lead guitar (tracks 14–16)
Bob Scott drums (tracks 14–16)
Jimmy Bowles piano (track 15)

■ THE TUNES
1 'I Feel Like Singing'
2 'News From Up The Street'
3 'Where's The Money?'
4 'The Buzzard Was Their Friend'
5 'Reelin' Down'
6 'Dig A Little Deeper'
7 'Canned Music'
8 'Walkin' One And Only'
9 'The Innocent Bystander'
10 'I Scare Myself'
11 'Presently In The Past'
12 'You Gotta Believe'
13 'I'm An Old Cowhand (From The Rio Grande)'
14 'My Old Timey Baby'
15 'Sweetheart (Waitress In A Donut Shop)'
16 ''Long Come A Viper'

I SCARE MYSELF

EARLY MUSES (1998)
DAN HICKS

This compendium of Dan's earliest recordings, compiled by Alec Palao, opens with an eleven-year-old Dan doing a brief duet with his father in 1953 on 'Home On The Range'; they get through a verse of the song and take a creditable crack at singing in harmony, then Dan's dad departs. The rest of the tracks here, recorded in approximately 1968, are uneven and extremely low-tech, and you can hear Dan working to find his style and figure out how to flesh it out. In other words, *Early Muses* is for aficionados only.

The first tune, 'Waitin' For The 103,' is a surprise in terms of how developed Dan already sounded as a vocalist. He was approximately twenty-seven years old when he made this recording, and his voice has a seasoned authority that belies his years. This is just one track, though, and he sounds less sure of himself on others. Dan has commented that he was going through a depression when he wrote several of the songs here, and you can hear that in some of them. 'Shall I Ask An Elf?,' 'Fallin' Apart,' 'Living With A Lie,' 'All-Day Sucker,' and 'The Gypsy's Secret'—these are *sad* songs, and it bears noting that Dan left them behind and never performed them live. He sure could write from the start, though! Some of his greatest songs date from this period, including 'The Innocent Bystander' and 'My Old Timey Baby.' 'Canned Music' is here, too, and it stands out like a diamond, even though the version here is thin. Play the version on this record, then listen to the version on *Where's The Money?*, and you'll be amazed by how quickly Dan got up to speed.

■ THE PERSONNEL
Dan Hicks vocals, guitar, Autoharp, banjo, harmonica, percussion
David LaFlamme violin
Jaime Leopold acoustic bass (tracks 3–6, 14, 16)
Jon Weber guitar (tracks 2 and 7)

■ THE TUNES
1 'Home On The Range' (by Kelley/Higley)
2 'Waitin' For The 103'
3 'How Can I Miss You When You Won't Go Away?'
4 'Slow Movin''
5 'Shorty Goes South'
6 'The Innocent Bystander'
7 'The Jukies' Ball'
8 'Euphonious Whale'
9 'He Don't Care'
10 'The Gypsy's Secret'

215

DAN HICKS

BEATIN' THE HEAT (2000)
DAN HICKS & THE HOT LICKS
Produced by Gary Hoey and Dave Kaplan.

This is one of Dan's most wonderful records. Marking his return to the studio after a twenty-year hiatus, *Beatin' The Heat* was his first release on Surfdog Records, which continued to be his label for the remainder of his life. Including several duets with an all-star cast, *Beatin' The Heat* also unveiled a handful of new Dan Hicks tunes that are among his best, including 'My Cello' and 'I Don't Want Love.' Dan pairs up with Rickie Lee Jones for a beautiful version of 'Driftin',' and he and Tom Waits have a blast trading vocal lines on 'I'll Tell You Why That Is,' a song about two clueless know-it-alls. It's a funny recording, and Dan and Waits dissolve into laughter at the end of the take. Another new tune, 'Strike It While It's Hot,' is a fabulous song that pairs Dan with American treasure Bette Midler, and the results are stunning. 'Strike It While It's Hot' is one of the most hopeful songs Dan ever wrote, and is quite moving for that reason. Also here is an anti-hippie song Dan wrote when hippies were crowding the streets of his Haight-Ashbury neighborhood circa 1966; the song is called 'He Don't Care,' and you can see a clip of Dan performing it while sitting on a park bench in the Haight in the 1968 documentary *Revolution*. Dan was a product of the Haight, but he was never a hippie; he was a hipster, and there's a big difference between the two. Another highlight here is a delightful cover of the American standard 'Hummin' To Myself'; Dan didn't write the tune, but it fits him to a *T*.

■ THE STORY
So, what'd ya write first? The music or the words? Actually, it's the words. I usually write the words for ten or fifteen songs. Then about fifteen melodies are written.

I SCARE MYSELF

Then they are thrown together into a hat and random pairings are made. This is the way the original songs for this recording came into being. And each tells at least one story. 'My Cello,' possibly torn from the pages of *Police Gazette*, experiences a hero who just can't seem to get to first base with the object of his affection, no matter how well he paints his own picture. The original singer of 'I Don't Want Love' never did get married but ended up weighing 376lbs. And 'I Scare Myself,' under the guise of a love ballad, tackles the military-industrial complex which is eating at our society even as we speak. It's obvious. But the corner is turned in 'Strike It While It's Hot,' which advises one to seize the opportunity to change things for the better. The song 'He Don't Care' takes a look at a character who may or may not exist; but if he does, please don't give him my phone number. The tempo jumps up a bit on 'Meet Me On The Corner,' which sounds like somebody is losing their grip and is desperately trying to reach out and touch somebody. What we need in this world is 'more confidence' and 'I'll Tell You Why That Is' lets you know that you're dealing with a man capable of explaining anything and everything, and maybe in the sequel tune he will actually do that! 'Doin' It!,' of course, has the same broad perspective as the Holland Tunnel in its relentless dedication to Cherchez la Femme. Time to 'chill' with 'Driftin'.' This song depicts a little respite from the cares of daily concerns, where the mind does its own boundless wandering. 'Hell I'd Go!' was written following the 'big scare' a while back when a small colony of earth-like persons were found to be living on the planet Pluto. You saw that article, didn't you? 'Don't Stop The Meter, Mack' warns of the consequences of infidelity, inspired by a scene from the movie *Taxi Driver*, or was it *Pee-Wee's Big Adventure*? The words came easy for 'I've Got A Capo On My Brain,' for it is based on an actual case history reported in 1956 of a folk/blues guitarist from Lousabaloosa, Louisiana. To extract the capo the patient's entire head had to be removed, apparently. I must add that the other songs on this disc were discovered in an old trunk in an attic above an abandoned pawnshop in Dusty Mouth, Montana. I've added a few words here and there, and I like the way they go. Little known facts: The subject of 'The Piano Has Been Drinking' finally got into rehab and has a steady job at Disneyland and the 'Hummin' To Myself' person was another loner but eventually joined a Hare Krishna all-boys choir. And 'The Chattanooga Shoe-Shine Boy' is now the Chattanooga Shoe-Shine Man and owns seventeen square blocks of prime location in downtown Chattanooga, Tennessee. And me? I humbly await my next assignment. But right now, here's *Beatin' The Heat*, a collection of songs and performances made

217

DAN HICKS

possible by Surfdog Records and Mr. Dave Kaplan, who tells me he has been some kind of fan for a long time. ('And let's bring back The Hot Licks—it's magical!') As he handed me that blank check and said, 'Let's make a record,' I knew that the gods of All-Things-Possible had smiled on me once again.

■ THE PERSONNEL

Dan Hicks vocals, rhythm guitar

Sid Page violin

Kevin Smith upright bass

Gregg Bissonette drums

Tom Mitchell guitar

Jessica Harper vocals

Karla DeVito vocals

■ THE TUNES

1 'My Cello'
2 'I Don't Want Love' (with Brian Setzer)
3 'I Scare Myself' (with Rickie Lee Jones)
4 'Strike It While It's Hot' (with Bette Midler)
5 'He Don't Care'
6 'Meet Me On The Corner' (with Elvis Costello and Brian Setzer)
7 'I'll Tell You Why That Is' (with Tom Waits)
8 'Hummin' To Myself' (by Sammy Fain, Herbert Magidson, and Monty Siegel)
9 'Doin' It'
10 'The Piano Has Been Drinking (Not Me)' (by Tom Waits)
11 'Chattanooga Shoe Shine Boy' (by Faron Young)
12 'Driftin'' (with Rickie Lee Jones)
13 'Hell, I'd Go'
14 'Don't Stop The Meter, Mack'
15 'I've Got A Capo On My Brain'
16 'Living With A Lie' (additional track on Japanese release)

THE MOST OF DAN HICKS & HIS HOT LICKS (2001)
DAN HICKS & HIS HOT LICKS

A complicated compilation! The liner notes tell us, 'Sometime around 1991 the original mix-down tapes for the A-side of Epic's *Original Recordings* album were damaged, copied to a safety reel, and then scrapped. The substandard sonic quality of the remaining safety reel necessitated remixing tracks 1,3,4,5, and 8 from

218

the original 8-track session masters. Every care was taken to match the original stereo mixes. Tracks 10–16 had never been mixed down until now; again, every effort was made to create stereo mixes contemporary to the period of these hitherto unreleased recordings. Tracks 1–9 were produced by Bob Johnston. Tracks 10–16 were produced by Pete Welding.' All the songs here had been previously released in alternate versions.

■ THE PERSONNEL

Dan Hicks vocals, rhythm guitar, harmonica, drums

Jon Weber lead guitar

Sid Page violin

Jaime Leopold bull fiddle

Terry Wilson drums

Tina Gancher vocals, celeste, piano

Nicolee Dukes vocals

Maryann Price vocals

Sherry Snow vocals

■ THE TUNES

1 'How Can I Miss You When You Won't Go Away?'
2 'Waitin' For The 103'
3 'I Scare Myself'
4 'Evenin' Breeze'
5 'Canned Music'
6 'Milk Shakin' Mama'
7 'Slow Movin''
8 'Shorty Takes A Dive'
9 'The Jukie's Ball'
10 'Payday Blues'
11 'You Gotta Believe'
12 'My Old Timey Baby'
13 'Living With A Lie'
14 'He Don't Care'
15 'By Hook Or By Crook'
16 'News From Up The Street'

ALIVE & LICKIN' (2001)
DAN HICKS & THE HOT LICKS
Produced by Gary Hoey and Dave Kaplan.

A selection of live material from 2001, mostly recorded at the Iron Horse Music Hall in Northampton, Massachusetts, *Alive & Lickin'* includes one of Dan's greatest recorded vocals. His fluid and effortlessly beautiful version of the Imelda May tune 'Wild About My Lovin'' is a potent reminder of the fact that Dan was primarily a jazz artist. His

DAN HICKS

phrasing on the song is so inventive and cool, and the way he bends the melody is so original and sexy—it's nothing short of perfection. Dan was in good form the night they recorded this album in terms of his mood, and he's particularly funny; the version of 'Payday Blues' here is among his wittiest and most playful. It's the vocals on this album that command the most attention, however. Over the course of the last sixteen years of his life, Dan moved ever deeper into the American songbook, and several cuts here show him developing into a masterful interpreter of classic standards like Sam Stept and Charles Tobias's 'Comes Love.' The final flowering of Dan's genius was his development as a vocalist, and that's in evidence here.

■ THE PERSONNEL

Dan Hicks vocals, rhythm guitar, harmonica

Susan Rabin vocals, percussion

Annabelle Cruz vocals, percussion, second violin

Brian Godchaux lead violin, mandolin

Tom Mitchell lead guitar

Steve Alcott string bass

Debbie Kee vocals and percussion (tracks 7 and 8)

Dan Andrews string bass (tracks 7 and 8)

■ THE TUNES

1 'Intro: Alive & Lickin''
2 'Where's The Money?'
3 'I Got Mine'
4 'Shootin' Straight'
5 'How Can I Miss You When You Won't Go Away?'
6 'The Piano Has Been Drinking (Not Me)' (by Tom Waits)
7 'My Cello'
8 'Wild About My Lovin'' (by Imelda May)
9 'I Feel Like Singin''
10 'Comes Love' (by Lew Brown, Sammy H. Stept, and Charles Tobias)
11 'Payday Blues'
12 'Caravan/Four Brothers' (by Juan Tizol / Jon Hendricks and James Guffre)
13 'Four Or Five Times'
14 'The Buzzard Was Their Friend'

I SCARE MYSELF

FEATURING AN ALL-STAR CAST OF FRIENDS (2003)
DAN HICKS & THE HOT LICKS
Produced by Daniel E. Catullo III and Dave Kaplan.

This CD/DVD set documents a show at San Francisco's Warfield Theater on December 12, 2001, presented in celebration of Dan's sixtieth birthday, that reunited him with virtually every musician he'd ever played with. More than forty players turn up here, including all the surviving members of The Charlatans, the classic Hot Licks lineup in their first reunion in more than two decades, vocal quartet The Fabulous Opinions, and musicians from Dan's teenage years.

The most remarkable thing about this recording is that it exists! Dan ran an *extremely* tight ship in terms of the level of musicianship he demanded from those he worked with, and there's no way he could do much quality control playing live with dozens of people, many of whom had never even met each other and were playing together for the first time. Dan rolled with it, though, and clearly had a great time. 'How Can I Miss You When You Won't Go Away?' proves to be well suited to a (giant) group sing-along, 'Payday Blues' sounds like a musical brawl, and the classic Hot Licks lineup delivers a solid version of 'Evenin' Breeze.' It's impressive that the massive cast here even attempted 'The Buzzard Was Their Friend,' a tricky song with complicated time that's hard for a well-rehearsed band to play, much less a crowd of forty people. Everyone on board manages to keep up and performs surprisingly well. Dan always had the profile of a loner, but this recording shows that he had a lot of friends.

■ THE PERSONNEL

Dan Hicks vocals, guitar
Louis Aissen flute, tenor sax
Alex Baum string bass, acoustic bass guitar
Dave Bell guitar
Stevie Black mandolin
Ned Boynton guitar
John Brandenburg vocals, guitar
Dick Bright violin
Joshua Brody accordion

Danny Caron guitar
Halimah Collingwood vocals, percussion
Annabelle Cruz vocals
Jay David vocals
Austin de Lone vocals, piano
Naomi Ruth Eisenberg vocals, violin
Gus Garelick violin
John Girton guitar
Brian Godchaux violin

221

DAN HICKS

Brien Hopkins vocals

George Hunter Autoharp, tambourine

David La Flamme violin

Jaime Leopold string bass

Paul Mehling guitar

Nils Molin string bass, percussion

Jack O'Hara vocals

Richard Olsen tenor sax, flute, clarinet, vocal

Sid Page violin

Maryann Price vocals, percussion

Susan Rabin vocals, percussion, ukulele

Josh Riskin drums, percussion

Paul Robinson guitar

David Rose string bass

Padma Rutley vocals

Richard Saunders string bass

Bob Scott drums, percussion

Mark Shinbrott piano

Julian Smedley violin

Paul Smith string bass

Turtle VanDeMarr guitar

Tim Vaughan drums, percussion

Jon Weber guitar

Mike Wilhelm guitar, vocals

Mitch Wood piano

Dick Ziegler vocals, guitar

■ THE TUNES

1 'You Gotta Believe'
2 'Milk Shakin' Mama'
3 'Waitin''
4 'Strike It While It's Hot'
5 'News From Up The Street'
6 'Walkin' One And Only'
7 'Evenin' Breeze'
8 'Canned Music'
9 'How Can I Miss You When You Won't Go Away?'
10 'Saving My Lovin''
11 'Payday Blues'
12 'I Scare Myself'
13 'The Buzzard Was Their Friend'
14 'Reelin' Down' (DVD bonus track)

SELECTED SHORTS (2004)
DAN HICKS & THE HOT LICKS
Produced by Tim Hauser and Dave Kaplan.

This is an odd one. The original plan was for Tim Hauser of The Manhattan Transfer to produce the album. This seems like a natural pairing, but by all reports the collaboration didn't go well, and the record has a disjointed feeling that's atypical of Dan's albums. Several of the songs reflect Dan's affection for Bob Wills, and are rooted in western swing; this is particularly true of 'That's Where I Am,' as well as Dan's duet with Willie Nelson on the Allan Jacobs tune 'One More Cowboy.' Flourishes of harmonica underscore the western vibe.

Also here is a stellar cover of 'I'll See You in My Dreams' that would do Django Reinhardt proud, and a swinging version of 'C'mon-A-My-House.' Studio versions of three songs—'Willie,' 'Barstool Boogie,' and 'Texas Kinda' Attitude'—from Dan's out-of-print live album, *Shootin' Straight*, are here, too, along with a hilarious new song, 'Hey Bartender,' and a lovely new ballad, 'Cue The Violins.' The most surprising cut is a duet on 'That Ain't Right' with Gibby Haynes of punk band The Butthole Surfers. Gibby's vocal was recorded over the phone.

■ THE PERSONNEL

Dan Hicks vocals, rhythm guitar
Jim Keltner drums
Tony Garnier bass
Sid Page violin
Gonzalo Bergara gypsy guitar

Bobbi Page vocals
Terry Wood vocals
Susan Rabin vocals
Robyn Seyler vocals

Special guests
Mike Finnigan Hammond B3
Van Dyke Parks accordion
Jack Sheldon trumpet
Jimmy 'Z' Zavala blues harmonica

Willie Nelson vocals
Jimmy Buffett vocals
Gibby Haynes vocals

Additional musicians
Denny Freeman guitar
Dave Bell rhythm guitar
Chuck Kavooras electric guitar, dobro
Gary Hoey electric guitar
Jesus Florido second violin

Cliff Hugo bass
David Jackson piano
Brie Darling congas, percussion
Dave Darling percussion

■ THE TUNES
1 'Mama's Boy Blues'
2 'That's Where I Am'
3 'Hey Bartender'
4 'Willie'
5 'One More Cowboy' featuring Willie Nelson (by Allan Jacobs)

DAN HICKS

TANGLED TALES (2009)
DAN HICKS & THE HOT LICKS
Produced by Chris Goldsmith.
Recorded at the Plant, Sausalito, California.

Tangled Tales is a mix of covers, new versions of five previously released songs, and three new tunes. The highlight of the record is Dan's beautiful cover of the Horace Silver tune 'Song For My Father.' This is a very special song and Dan—who loved his father deeply—infuses his rendition of it with a lot of heart. Also of interest is Dan's take on Dylan's pioneering rap tune, 'Subterranean Homesick Blues'; it's surprising to learn that Dan is one of thirteen artists who've covered this singularly unmusical tune. The title track is a new number and an exercise in pure scat, and another new tune, 'Let It Simmer' is a laid-back jazz number with a mellow vocal that's classic Hicks.

■ THE STORY
Tangled Tales (of titillation) calculated to keep your toes tappin' and your synapses zappin'. Yes, each song tells a tale. Some are gleeful and joyous; some pensive and reflective. Some both. But each tangled in a web of sharps and flats.

Take, for instance, 'A Magician,' a song that asks the question, 'Where did I go wrong?' Sometimes you only get one chance. Or perhaps the selection 'Who Are You?' which answers the query, 'Who is the baddest in the valley?' For those in need of temper modification you might pay attention to 'Let It Simmer!' and for those not in need of anything, the wordless 'Tangled Tales' will be perfect!

Of course, tales of romance abound! 'Savin' My Lovin'' elaborates on one very choosy individual. '13-D' states, in simple terms, that there's some big shoes to fill to sing this tune. 'The Rounder' is a case study of the free soul. Trying to be free is 'The Diplomat,' who echoes the sentiment 'Can't we all just get along?'

Another lesson in social conduct is 'Subterranean Homesick Blues,' which tells us to stay underground for the best results! 'Ragtime Cowboy Joe,' a song from 1912, is a tangled tale of man, beast, and syncopation. Film at Eleven. Deserving its own reality show is the song 'The Blues My Naughty Baby Gave To Me,' in which are listed seventeen ways to bring yourself down (or not). Genuine heroes are hard to come by, but 'Song For My Father' knows one for sure!

And while we're at it, give yourself a hand and please continue …

This CD is most auspicious to me in that it contains the title song of which I am duly proud. As a lyricist struggling for years to make syntax and meaning blend with poetry and rhythm, I take pride in weaving stories, messages, and characterizations that come out palatable to the listener (and myself). With the tune 'Tangled Tales' I have met all these criteria beyond any expectations! To me the words in the chorus alone embody my deepest DNA. My chest swells and my eyes tear to think that I have finally mastered the skill of lyric writing, and it rests with 'Tangled Tales.' Bah bey bah deet dot dooty! I am glad I was home when the muses called that day. I caution the listener not to read into this material, but embrace the sounds as you would when your mother called you in for more cookies. The words are printed here so that all may know the serenity this composition can bring to those brave enough to make the trek. Let's sing:

■ THE PERSONNEL

Dan Hicks vocals, rhythm guitar, percussion

Daria vocals

Roberta Donnay vocals

Dave Bell lead and rhythm guitar

Paul Smith string bass

Richard Chon violin, mandolin

Brian Simpson drums, percussion

David Grisman mandolin solo (tracks 2 and 4)

Richard Greene violin solo (tracks 1, 6, and 9)

Roy Rogers slide guitar solo (tracks 7 and 11)

Bruce Forman twelve-string guitar solo (track 4), guitar solo (track 6)

Charlie Musselwhite harmonica solo (tracks 1 and 7)

John Rosenberg piano (track 13)

Austin de Lone timpani (track 9), accordion (tracks 11 and 12)

John Hunter strings

DAN HICKS

■ THE TUNES

CRAZY FOR CHRISTMAS (2010)
DAN HICKS & THE HOT LICKS

Produced by Chris Goldsmith.
Recorded at Glenwood Place Studios, Burbank, California.

This is an album of Christmas music for people who hate Christmas music. For starters, all the songs are secular and focus on the fun of Christmas, as opposed to the stressful parts. Much of the music here has a western swing flavor, too, which has a built in fun factor. Surprisingly, the standout cut is Dan's interpretation of the Christmas standard 'Carol Of The Bells'; he devised a complex arrangement for the song that's built around scatting, and the results are lovely. There are four original Dan Hicks Christmas tunes, and adaptations of two standards he wrote new lyrics for that transformed them into groovy Christmas songs. Even groovier is his cover 'Cool Yule' by the inimitable Steve Allen. This is a Christmas album you can listen to all year round.

■ THE STORY

Once upon a time in a thick forest far far away there lived the Three Bears, in a home they had built themselves—a log cabin, much like the one Abraham Lincoln was raised in. One day they made themselves some chili for lunch and was gonna eat it on the back picnic table. So they set it out and went into the cabin to wash their

226

hands. And while they were inside along came a fella named the Big Bad Wolf—from the Three Little Pigs story. Well, the wolf saw all this chili and immediately scarfed up everything, because that was part of his personality.

When the bears discovered the crime the proper authorities were immediately notified. Assigned to the case was one Sgt. Humpty Dumpty, who was working part-time as the local constable and had yet to sit on any walls and fall down and bust himself up so bad. Dumpty was a Dick Tracy fan and didn't take any nonsense.

Now, up until this time the phenomenon known as 'Christmas' was not in practice on a world-wide scale and had a limited following in a small community settled in Nova Scotia. As a matter of fact only one person celebrated Christmas every December 25th—Walter Phillips and he thought he had a good thing going. Indeed he did; for the idea eventually caught on and the rest is history!

Oh, and the Big Bad Wolf? He was put on probation and he's somewhat changed his ways.

■ THE PERSONNEL

Dan Hicks vocals, rhythm guitar, percussion, harmonica

Daria vocals, kazoo

Roberta Donnay vocals, kazoo

Gonzalo Bergara rhythm and gypsy lead guitar

Ken Wild string bass

Greg Bissonette drums, percussion

John Rosenberg piano

Paul Smith bowed bass solo (track 4)

Dave Bell guitar solo (track 5)

■ THE TUNES

1 'Christmas Mornin'' (an adaptation of 'Where's The Money?')
2 'Santa Gotta Choo Choo' (an adaptation of 'Choo Choo Ch'Boogie' by Vaughn Horton, Denver Darling, and Milton Gabler)
3 'Somebody Stole My Santa Claus Suit' (an adaptation of 'Somebody Stole My Gal' by Leo Wood)
4 'Carol Of The Bells' (traditional)

5 'Run Run Rudolph' (by Johnny Marks and Marvin Brodie)
6 'Santa's Workshop'
7 'Old Fashioned Christmas'
8 'Cool Yule' (by Steve Allen)
9 'I've Got Christmas By The Tail'
10 'I Saw Mommy Kissing Santa Claus' (by Tommie Connor)
11 'Here Comes Santa Claus' (by Gene Autry and Oakley Haldeman)
12 'Under The Mistletoe'

DAN HICKS

LIVE AT DAVIES SYMPHONY HALL (2013)
DAN HICKS & THE HOT LICKS

Live show produced by SFJAZZ (Randall Kline, Laura Evans, and team) and Great Guns/Steep Productions Inc. (Clare Wasserman and Dan Hicks).

This is basically a Dan Hicks love-fest: a long list of great musicians joined him onstage for a show celebrating his seventieth birthday, and they all clearly adore him. Everybody really stretches out, too, on this series of extended live versions of some of his best-loved songs.

Highlights include a version of 'He Don't Care' that allows Dan to reveal how he really feels about hippies and street people. Jim Kweskin is on hand for 'Beedle Um Bum,' an old jug band tune that The Kweskin Jug Band covered in 1963; the version of the song here is terrific.

All of the guest artists are onstage for 'I Feel Like Singin',' and each of them takes a crack at scat singing. One imagines they did this at Dan's behest—he loved scatting—and many of them interweave their scatting with words of affection for him.

The grand finale of the show is a version of 'I Scare Myself' that emphasizes the Spanish underpinnings of the song. This is a mysterious, strangely beautiful song, charged with turbulent feeling, and it's fitting that the last cut on the last record Dan released is this expansive rendition of 'I Scare Myself.'

■ THE STORY

Louise M. Davies Symphony Hall was chosen by the San Francisco Jazz Fest to be the spot for my big birthday concert. The idea was to invite great fellow musical artists to the stage and do some tunes (mostly mine) for the folks! Here is a little re-cap of that evening … simply put, it was a sold-out crowd and we dazzled 'em for two and a half hours.

It began with the eight-piece Stage Band playing a medley of some of my recognizable melodies, during which I did a little dance. Then a bunch of vocal guests joined me as we did 'The Joint Is Jumpin'' and 'By Hook Or By Crook' (Roy Rogers—slide solo). This was followed by feature duets with Maria Muldaur, Ray Benson, and Rickie Lee Jones.

The original Hot Licks Band was introduced by Harry Shearer and we covered six numbers, with Dave Grisman on mandolin on one. The Stage Band hit the chaser 'Yardbird Suite' and we took a break.

228

I SCARE MYSELF

At the beginning of the second segment I was presented with a special plaque from the CA State Senate honoring the event. Nice.

Santa Rosa was my hometown, so an eight-piece combo was formed (with members going back to junior high) and we did a couple of swing instrumentals. Van Dyke Parks then introduced the current Hot Licks lineup and we broke into three tunes. At this point guitarist Bruce Forman and pianist Van Dyke Parks sat in on 'Song For My Father.'

Now it was time for the jug band influence and Jim Kweskin led us thru an old-timey number. And then onto acoustic blues with 'Cow-Cow Boogie' featuring Ramblin' Jack Elliott, Roy Rogers, John Hammond, Turtle VanDeMarr, Jim Kweskin, Ray Benson, and David Grisman, with Harry Shearer on string bass.

Straight-ahead jazz could not be left out so the Stage Band and guitarists Tuck and Bruce jammed with my new lyrics on 'Take The "A" Train.' The jamming thing kept going with everybody scatting on 'I Feel Like Singin'.' The chaser hit and we were gone! But were we? No! The entire cast (thirty-eight people) would not leave without pounding out the rhythms to the last big song, 'I Scare Myself,' with Benito Cortez, Turtle VanDeMarr, David Grisman, and Sid Page on solos.

It sounded to me like the audience by this time was in an altered state, but I, and most of the performers, had been that way all night!

This CD represents highlights of this concert, April 6, 2012, with everything chronological as it happened. Time necessitated leaving some things on the cutting room floor.

■ THE PERSONNEL

Original Hot Licks

Dan Hicks vocals, guitar

Sid Page mandolin, violin

Jon Weber guitar

Naomi Ruth Eisenberg vocals, violin

Maryann Price vocals, bird whistle

New Hot Licks

Dan Hicks guitar, vocals

Daria vocals, percussion, kazoo

Roberta Donnay vocals, percussion, kazoo

Paul Smith string bass

Benito Cortez violin, mando

Paul Robinson guitar

DAN HICKS

Hicksville Stage Band

Mike Rinta trombone

Tom Poole trumpet

Richard Olsen tenor sax, clarinet, flute

Charlie Gurke baritone sax, tenor

Brian Cooke piano

Paul Robinson guitar

Paul Smith string bass

Brian Simpson drums

Additional musical participants

Banana, Wayne Whittaker, Dennis Williams, Kent Benedict, Sandy Lane, Dick Ziegler, Sara Wasserman, John Brandeberg.

Vocal and instrumental guests

Ray Benson, Van Dyke Parks, Rickie Lee Jones, Maria Muldaur, Jim Kweskin, Turtle VanDeMarr, John Hammond, Tuck and Patti, Roy Rogers, David Grisman, Harry Shearer, Bruce Forman, Ramblin' Jack Elliott.

■ THE TUNES

1 'Overture Medley'

2 'By Hook Or By Crook'

3 'Dan's Welcome'

4 'Hummin' To Myself'

5 'Driftin''

6 'Evenin' Breeze'

7 'He Don't Care'

8 'Song For My Father' (by Horace Silver)

9 'Take The "A" Train' (by Billy Strayhorn)

10 'Beedle Um Bum' (by Rev. Thomas Dorsey)

11 'I Feel Like Singin',' with 'Yardbird Suite' chaser

12 'I Scare Myself'

end
credits

ACKNOWLEDGMENTS

Wow—the book is done!

My love and thanks to:

Kristine—there simply would be no book without her. She persevered with Dan, he trusted her and talked to her—no easy feat! Her name belongs on the cover with his and I pleaded and cajoled, but she always said no, it's Dan's story. It is truly her great effort and love that made it happen.

To my true loves, Sara, Steph, and Joan. I would not be on this planet today without you. The last couple of years were endurable because of your love, support, and fun!

To Dave and everyone over all the years at Surfdog Records, our musical home. Dave was and is Dan's champion and supported his vision unfailingly.

To Elvis and Tommy. I asked you to bookend Dan's words and you did it so beautifully. Many thanks.

To our band, Paul, Daria, Roberta, Benito, and Michael. Thanks for the love, commitment, and endless rehearsals always!

To my girls and boys—Rita, Ned and Chris, Larry, Terry, Jesse, Maria, Slim, Paul, Mark and Zoe, Jill, Jeanne, Kathee, Jaime and Sid, Kent, Erik, Dan and Janice, Bob and Leslie, Gregory, the Muffs, Marni and Shannon. I love you all.

And to our wonderful little town of Mill Valley, always a refuge, our happy home for decades. We had the greatest life together here.

And, to Dan's repertory company, the dear friends who helped make the music and art happen—Ken and Kathy, Megan, Barry and Eva at WIGT, Lucy, Steve, Edwin and Tim at the Throck, Leslie and Tony. Jeff, Anne Marie, Toni, and everyone in Madison.

To Tom and Nigel at Jawbone Press in London, our book's lucky home!

Gotta thank all the dogs, Fetch, Barney, Pebbles, Sami, Luccy, Wylie, Bianca, and the magnificent Coco.

DAN HICKS

Lastly, Joe's Taco Lounge and d'Angelo's for all the last-minute late night take out dinner orders!

Dan would periodically look over at me and say, 'You know, WE are the great love affair of the century; it's not Taylor and Burton, it's US!' I would always respond with a laugh and say, 'Yeah, yeah …' He never liked that and would say, 'No, you don't get it—it's us!'

Now I say to my darling warrior husband, YES, you were right. I love you madly and forever.

C.T. HICKS, MILL VALLEY, CALIFORNIA, JANUARY 2017

My first thanks go to Clare Wasserman for all that she gave Dan, the love and the home and the hope and the inspiration. We had Dan with us much longer than we would've were it not for her.

Thanks also to Elvis Costello and Tommy LiPuma for their eloquent words about Dan, and to Lorraine Wild for her inspired early vision of the book. Tony Manzella and Rusty Sena made the scans affordable, and filmmaker Matt Mays contributed to the momentum—thanks Matt.

Respect to Alec Palao for his scholarship on Dan, thanks to Matt Groening for the support and to Dave Kaplan for putting Dan's records out, and much gratitude to the great photographers who contributed pictures to the book: J.D. Crayne and Barry Toranto made particularly generous gifts of their work, and a BIG thank you to Herb Greene for his amazing photos. Herb was kind of the sixth Charlatan. He shot all the fantastic photos of the band, and is one of the unsung heroes of the Haight.

A big thank you to Tom Seabrook and Nigel Osborne for recognizing Dan as the great artist that he is, and publishing this book.

Thanks most of all to Dan for the many gifts he gave. Weren't we lucky to have him?

KRISTINE McKENNA, LOS ANGELES, CALIFORNIA, JANUARY 2017

PHOTO CREDITS

All photographs from the author's collection, except: **4** *Elvis Costello and Dan Hicks in downtown Mill Valley, 2015*, photograph by Lesley Delone; **39**, **52** photographs by Herb Greene; **53** *top left* designed by George Hunter, *bottom left* artwork by

I SCARE MYSELF

Lee Conklin, *right* photograph by Herb Greene; **54** designed by Rick Griffin; **54–55** photographs by Herb Greene; **56** *top* artwork by Alton Kelly, *bottom* photograph by Herb Greene; **58** *top* artwork by George Hunter; **59–63**, **64** *bottom*, **104** photographs by Herb Greene; **105** *top* artwork by George Hunter; **108–109** photographs by Herb Greene; **110–111**, **128** photographs by Jonathan Perry; **167** photograph by J.D. Crayne; **179** photograph by Jonathan Perry; **180–183** photographs by Barry Toranto; **184** photograph by Stephanie Clarke; **185** photograph by Dan Hicks; **188–189** photograph by Barry Toranto; **190–192** photographs by J.D. Crayne; **198** *Tommy LiPuma and Dan Hicks at Chasen's Restaurant in Los Angeles, 1973*, photograph courtesy of Tommy LiPuma. Every effort has been made to contact copyright holders, but if you feel there has been a mistaken attribution, please contact the publishers.

ENDNOTES

1 'Dewey Defeats Truman' was a legendarily incorrect headline in the *Chicago Tribune*.

2 The 4-H Club is a youth organization founded by the US government in 1902 and dedicated to 'engaging youth to reach their fullest potential.' Originally conceived to instruct rural youth in farming practices, it subsequently expanded its programs to include science and the arts.

3 The reverse officers' training corps.

4 In June 1964, three members of the Student Non-Violent Coordinating Committee, James Chaney, Andrew Goodman, and Michael Schwerner, were abducted and murdered in an apparent racially motivated incident in Nebosha County, Mississippi.

Hicks and Ziegler were traveling through the state during Freedom Summer, when 700 students from around the US traveled to Mississippi to register black voters.

5 The song is actually 'I'm So Glad,' and James was in fact sixty-two at the time.

6 Also known as the Bear, Owsley Stanley III was the first independent chemist to make mass quantities of LSD during the 60s, and he played a crucial role in the San Francisco counterculture of the period. Between 1965 and 1967 he produced more than ten million doses of the drug, most of which he distributed for free.

index

ALSO AVAILABLE IN PRINT AND EBOOK
EDITIONS FROM JAWBONE PRESS

NEW FOR 2017